Happy New Year — To A
Wonderful Mother-In-Law —
Love, Sherry

Postmark
Vermont

Marguerite Hurrey Wolf

THE NEW ENGLAND PRESS
Shelburne, Vermont

For Patty and Debbie
With admiration and love.

Cover illustration by John MacKimmie
First Edition
Library of Congress Catalog Card Number: 94-61332
ISBN: 1-881535-12-6

For additional copies of this book or for a catalog of our other New England titles, please write:

The New England Press, Inc.
P.O. Box 575
Shelburne, Vermont 05482

"What's Good about January?" and "The Bare Bones of November" were originally published in *The Burlington Free Press.*

Printed in the United States of America

Contents

Dramatis Personae

Any resemblance to actual people in this book is entirely intentional. They are my family and friends, the same ones I've been writing about for twenty-nine years in ten books, with one major exception. We now have to manage without George, who died in 1990. He is still with us in many ways. We talk about him all the time, and sometimes we can't believe he isn't still here.

The changes are most obvious in the grandsons, Patrick, eighteen, Peter, sixteen, and Morgan, thirteen. All three are big, blond, and beautiful, and in the way of adolescents, occasionally embarrassed by their handsome, caring, intelligent, forty-something parents, Tage and Patty Strom and Steve and Debbie Page. The boys don't voice their chagrin about me partly because they are polite and partly because it is my prerogative as a grandmother to be a slightly weird relic of another time. They all share my love of Vermont.

They are my link with the future and I am their link with the past, a symbiotic and mutually enlightening relationship.

A SENSE OF PLACE

Karen Blixen wrote, "I am in a place where I ought to be."
Me too.

She was writing about Africa, where she felt a natural rapport
with the native tribesmen and the flora and fauna on her coffee
plantation. I am writing about Jericho, Vermont, a totally different ecology, with the same sense of belonging to this small wooded
piece of land in the foothills of the Green Mountains. The flam-
ing maples in the fall, the tall tamarack that lifts its golden candle
above the waterfall, the foaming shadbushes throughout the woods
in the spring are all old friends.

On a trip to Viscaya, the ornate estate near Miami, the gardens
intimidated me with tropical, visceral-looking roots and inter-
twining vines. I admire the color of flamingos, but a motionless
blue heron in my pool beneath the waterfall is a living Japanese
scroll. This morning a doe was standing in the shallow water at

1

the edge, drinking. She looked up at me and for a long moment we studied each other with interest before she bounded off into the bushes.

My peripatetic chickadees, tame enough to snatch sunflower seeds from my hand, and the red squirrel hanging upside down to gorge upon the seeds in the bird feeder, are my daily companions. Even the weasel with whom I feuded over the chickens turned into the most beautiful snow white ermine when the snow fell. I would have happily shared my space with him if he had only preyed upon the meadow mice instead of my hens.

When I am in another country or even in another state I get homesick for Vermont. I wasn't born here but ever since we bought the little old house next door in 1948 we have put down those tenacious taproots which a transplant sends down even deeper than a native.

A sense of place is the accumulation of memories. Debbie and Patty learned to swim in our pool. Last summer I looked down and saw my grandsons rearranging the rocks to dam the pool just as every male from four to ninety-four has felt the urge to do ever since we' ve been here. It saddens me to see pasture that once nourished several sheep and geese becoming overgrown with goldenrod and brambles, but it' s no longer sensible for me to keep farm animals, to carry 100-pound grain bags, and skid up and down the path to the barn in the wintertime.

A few days after they had been married in Finland, Patty and Tage's wedding reception was held here on this porch, on a day so hot that the guests and the wedding cake melted in unison.

Debbie and Steve were married down at the brook, on a grassy spot with the waterfall as a backdrop. It was an October day when the foliage was at its peak, but the rainfall was too. The waterfall turned into Niagara, and the guests wore boots and raincoats.

It seemed right to bury George's ashes down by the brook also, on a flat raised spot above the pool. It is a place where he liked to shoot at targets with a .22. Water had never crept up that high, even after the wildest flood of snowmelt in April. But a few days after the girls and grandsons and I had buried George's ashes, we had a flash flood of monsoon proportions. I sloshed down the path and saw that the swirling, muddy water was eddying over the burial site. I had to tell the girls and was apprehensive about their reactions, but to my relief, they both responded with a mixture of sadness and laughter.

"Pop always said that he didn't care, that we could throw his ashes in Lake Champlain." And now they may have been carried tumbling over the rocks of Mill Brook, past the farms bordering the Winooski River, through the gorges and into Lake Champlain. He would have enjoyed retracing this last journey.

We have planted and harvested gardens here for forty-five years in harmony and combat with nature. We have chased pigs and sheep and geese who chronically yearned for greener pastures.

It was here in this house that George quietly slept away. The best and worst times in our fifty-one years of marriage happened here, even though we had only lived year-round here for twenty years. They are still happening. This is where I know I should be.

YEARNING FOR GREEN

It is March 12. There are eighteen inches of snow on the ground, and it has been snowing gently off and on for the last three days. Last night the temperature dropped to zero, and the weatherman says we are going to get the mother of all storms, one to two feet of snow tomorrow.

It is beautiful with frosted evergreens and wide expanses of unblemished snow that would sparkle in the sun if we had any sun. Debbie, Steve, and Morgan ski on the mountain every weekend, and on Jim McCullough's cross country trails outside their door most late afternoons. I should be happy for them and for the many Vermonters who enjoy or profit from the snow, but the fact is I am yearning for spring.

I find myself hunting for its least intimation. The lengthening days and the welcome light reassure me that we are headed in the right direction. There is a nuthatch at the feeder. That's a good sign. There have also been several wasps staggering around on the windowsill. Why are wasps so hard to kill? One swat does in a fly but a wasp has more lives than a cat. Flower and vegetable seeds and Easter candies are on display in the stores, but products for sale are always far ahead of the season. There is an enormous chocolate Easter bunny at Snowflake Chocolates for $49.53. The seeds I sent away for have arrived, but even the peas and radishes won't get out of their packets for another six weeks.

This hunger for green is as predictable as the rise of sap in the maple trees. They should occur simultaneously, but with our present heavy cover of snow and recent below-zero temperatures, the maples aren't ready to share their wealth. The late night TV news showed Governor Dean tapping a maple on the lawn of the capitol, but in spite of the encouragement of a small crowd and the cameramen, no drop dripped until an hour later.

Asparagus at the supermarket is reasonably priced, and in spite of telling myself that in two months I'll be eating my own asparagus twice a day, I did succumb. It was slender and had tolerated its long trip pretty well, but it harbored more than the memory of the sandy soil of its origin. When I was a child, if I complained of grit in spinach, my mother quoted her grandmother, who used to say, "Swallow it and put it on your backbone!"

Mud season should have started with town meeting last week, but instead of the usual complaints about bottomless mud and frost heaves, the argument was over the amount of salt being used to keep us on the roads instead of in the ditches.

I'm tempted to dig down through the snow covering the flower beds to see if the first pale daffodil spears have broken through.

They probably have, since on the lawn of the Brownell Library in Essex Junction I thought I saw something green. I squatted down and peered eagerly at the tiny green and white spike.

"Did you lose something?" a deep voice behind me asked.

"No, I think I found something: crocus leaves!"

The startled expression on his face turned into a wide grin.

"You mean you believe that there WILL be spring this year?"

The lengthening days have sent a message of light down through the snow to the dormant bulbs. And even though I'm not covered with snow, the same light is telling me not to despair. I'll hear the geese some day before too long, and finally the peepers will be singing their sleighbell love songs at the brook. There are times when Vermonters have to live on faith.

THE BLIZZARD OF '93

My mother often had told me about the blizzard of 1888 when she was an eight-year-old schoolgirl. I envied that exciting experience, and at that same age I welcomed every snowstorm, hoping for the double bonanza of no school and drifts high enough for a snow fort or an igloo. I remember one dramatic storm in Montclair, New Jersey, in the twenties when a solid crust formed on top of deep snow and we could skid around, exploring the unfamiliar raised terrain of undulating valleys and peaks.

We had a few impressive storms during the years we lived in South Burlington in the fifties. I remember one time when Homer Dubois's plow could no longer clear a swath wide enough in our long driveway. In the middle of the night a huge earth mover lumbered down our lane like a prehistoric monster with great glowing yellow eyes, scooping up mouthfuls of snow and spewing them out over the fields.

But not until March 13, 1993, (Patty's birthday) did I feel the power and majesty of "the blizzard of the century." It was a child's dream, but a dichotomy of admiration and apprehension for an older woman living alone. I was already twitchy about the foot of snow on the roof, and the threat of two or three more feet made me watch the beams nervously.

It began very gently, with misty snow sifting down in the late morning. The radio had been warning us all morning about the massive storm that was moving up the entire East Coast, paralyzing southern states with a foot of snow, and closing Philadelphia and the Pennsylvania turnpike. A gauzy curtain of snow fell softly all early afternoon, but by nightfall the wind had picked up, and swirls of snow were eddying and leaping around the house. When I looked out the west window, the barn was only dimly visible. By evening, waves of blowing snow danced and twirled in the porch light, ebbing and flowing like the pulsations of northern lights. All night I could hear the hissing crescendos spitting against the house.

In the welcome light of morning it was still snowing and blowing. Waves of fallen snow were cresting and sending plumes across the driveway. The whole outside world was in constant motion. The evergreens were laden, but when the wind swooped near them, they released masses of snow that joined in the hectic dance. There was no sound of cars on the road all night except for the muted rumble of the snow plow. It was impossible to open either my front or back door. Snow was as high as the window sills on the south side. I shoved the front door open a crack and squeezed the shovel out, pushing the light snow gradually away until I could inch outside and open the door freely. Cary Todriff came to plow the driveway, and the drifts he pushed up were higher than my head.

Finally the snowfall petered out. Debbie and Steve came over in the truck and shovelled a path from the door to the driveway. It was almost a tunnel, five feet high on each side. The snow on the roof was three feet deep in places. I kept hoping the wind would blow some of it off. It's a new roof, well insulated, in fact so well insulated that nothing melts. Ours is the only house not ornamented with long silver needles of icicles. But could the roof tolerate the weight? To ease my anxiety, Steve said that a cubic foot of snow weighing forty pounds would be a threat. So he got a tape measure and cut a twelve-inch cube of snow, stood on my weighing machine, at first solo, and then with his snowy burden. It weighed twenty pounds. I stopped worrying. We had another five inches of snow the next day but the roof, and my peace of mind, stayed intact.

At Desso's store everyone had a story to tell. One man had fallen off his roof, cars were buried, the airport closed, sections of the interstate were closed, no *New York Times*. It was a matter of pride to report the deepest snow. If you said the drifts were six feet high at your house, the man in earmuffs snorted that his were ten feet high. There was a camaraderie in sharing this struggle of fragile man against the fury of nature. Milton wrote "That which purifies us is trial." We had not only survived, we had helped each other and triumphed. We had stayed warm and centered down unscathed by the great white horses of winter pounding through our valley.

And now our grandchildren can regale their children with their no-doubt embellished memories of the blizzard of '93.

NOTHING
BUT THE TRUTH

If you want an honest opinion, ask a third- or fourth-grader. The spelling may surprise you because they spell a word the way they hear it, having heard words more often than they have read them.

Every year Debbie asks me to come and talk to her class at the Flynn School, either about Vermont flora and fauna or, like this year, to encourage writing. They had invited local writers to talk about their craft and hopefully remove the hocus-pocus from writing for publication.

The fringe benefits of these encounters are the letters the children are asked to write to the presenter. Some are the usual "thank you for coming" letters written under duress, but now and then a special interest shows through. They are reproduced here just the way they were written.

"Dear Mrs. Wolf, I wish I was a writer like you. If I was a writer like you I would write about me. I like Mrs. Page a lot and you and Mrs. Page (Debbie) would make a great team if you would write a book together."

Or another: "Thank you for sharing those storys. I liked the one where your daughter said the goat was making raizins on the seet of the car."

Jamie wrote: "I love your story about Mrs. Page. Writhing is my favorite subjeck. I wish thar was more writhing. I am writhing 20 Megu Lise."

"I rely apreshet you coming. Thank you rely moch."

Krystie drew a tulip and under it wrote: "You did a lot of expression on the books. Your welcome to come again any time you want."

Molly was more interested in the refreshments. "I'm glad you came. I liked the cookies."

Sophie, whose mother was also a presenter, wrote: "You sure talked about cats a lote! But you discribed them well."

At the end of the session one little boy waved his arm nearly out of its socket wanting to ask a question. Did he want to know how I wrote, or perhaps tell a story about his pet? Nope.

The moment I called on him he asked, "How old are you?"

I said I was very old and told him my age.

"That's nothing. My grandmother is 95!"

But my all-time favorite fourth-grade comment was made quite a few years ago in the Jericho Elementary School. A small boy studied the flattering picture of me on the dust jacket of my first book. It had been taken years ago by Bachrach.

"Is that supposed to be you?"

"Yes."

"Well, you sure were better looking in the olden days!"

THE SIXTH SENSE
OF SPRING

When does spring arrive in Vermont? Forget about the groundhog in Punxsutawney, Pennsylvania. On February 2 in Jericho, the woodchuck is so sound asleep that you could dig him out and toss him around like a furry basketball without eliciting any response at all.

The vernal equinox and the arrival of spring rarely coincide in Vermont. But the winter-weary Vermonter eagerly seeks out the merest hints of renewal. It's arrival is nothing spectacular like what you would see in the azalea gardens of South Carolina, the dogwoods of the Ozarks, or the laurel in the Great Smokies. Spring is tentative in Vermont, appearing shyly on the south side of the house, while scraps of snow and winter still cling to the north side. You have to hunt for the earliest portents. The osiers at the roadside glow a deeper crimson. Buds on the lilac bushes grow fatter and turn green. Buckets sprout on the maple trees, the crows come out of the woods, and the chickadees change their tune from "Chickadee-dee-dee" to "Spring soon."

I walk out to the mailbox one morning in March and hear a distant sound that evokes some atavistic memory. It is the far-off honking of geese flying north. I scan the whole sky and finally make out the V-shaped skein, so high that it is just an irregular string of black beads. The "hounds of heaven," as they've been called, are as sure a sign of spring as the hub-deep mud on our back roads. Why does this wild call move us so deeply? Was it a symbol of spring that quickened the pulse of our ancient ancestors?

The smells of spring are subtle too: the faint maple fragrance of the steam billowing out of the sugarhouse when the sap is boiling, the leaf mold smell of the earth when the granular snow shrinks back in the garden.

It will be more than a month before daffodils bloom, but their green spears already thrust through the snow, impaling a leaf or two. And the determined little snowdrops, so fragile looking, but as dependable as the pussy willows fluffing out their furry buds in the swamp, poke through the icy crust, undeterred by alternate rain and sleet.

Shut your eyes and you can hear spring in the snowmelt dripping from the eaves, in the "okalee" of the first male redwings staking out their territories before the females follow, and in our brook as it cascades over the rocks and plunges into the pool.

And then there is another sense, a restlessness and urgency, the energy of renewed life, the urge to open the windows and hang the laundry outdoors where it can flap and shout back at the wind.

This restlessness evokes other springs. My recurrent spring memory is of Geneva, Switzerland, when I was seven years old. My older sister was busy and happy in school, but I was so miserable with a teacher who thought that if she shouted I might understand French that I was allowed to stay home. It was a relief not to be called "méchante." I knew what "méchante" was. It was "bad," "rude," as all American children were considered to be. I wasn't deaf, I was stricken dumb. I think if I were to smell the mixture of chalk, carpet slippers (so that we would make no noise), and thick chunks of bread and chocolate for recess again, I would still feel afraid.

Once I was out of that school, life became very pleasant again. I had reading lessons with my grandmother, played Double Canfield with my grandfather, and had a weekly art lesson with one of the many pale, weepy, white Russian ladies who filled the garrets of Paris and Geneva in post World War I Europe. I also became the constant companion of Olga Hausmann, our German-Swiss maid.

Why I wasn't equally dumb with Olga, I don't know. She knew almost no English when she came to us, and I knew no German, but we communicated somehow. I remember that we chattered endlessly in the kitchen. Perhaps our mutual shortcomings drew us together. We were both foreigners, awkward and sensitive. She would burst into tears every time she dropped a plate, but would break another the next day. That seemed perfectly natural to me. I was awkward too. I would scramble up onto a chair to grind coffee beans in a little mill that was attached to the wall, and I often spilled a good deal of the ground coffee out of its little drawer as I jumped down.

That was the dominant smell of that kitchen, freshly ground coffee, and the soup that Olga kept simmering in a marmite. Whenever I see an old recipe that says, "throw in a handful of shelled peas," I remember Olga's soup. She was the only person I've ever known who did throw in the ingredients. She would stand at the iron sink, wash the vegetables, and toss a handful of leeks or carrots across the room into the soup pot. I admired her skill. She also scraped most leftovers from our dinner plates into the pot. I wondered then, and still do, at my mother's naïveté. I would hear her boast to a friend, "I don't know what Olga makes the soup from. She must scrape the kitchen table." Not the table, I thought, but the plates, a dab of mashed potatoes, a chop bone, bits of salad, part of a roll; they all went into the big marmite of potage, so that our kitchen had the delicious variety of smells of a restaurant.

Two or three times a week Olga and I went to the market, she with a string bag and I with my retired school bag over my shoulder. We went early and spent the entire morning leisurely absorbing the colors and smells of the market. There was no refrigeration so all the meats were cut from carcasses while you waited. Could a child today ever know the satiny texture and royal color of a whole beef liver, or the excitement when the butcher plunged his hand into a fowl and drew out eggs in various stages of development, even one with the shell already on? The butchers outdid each other in offering samples of liverwurst and other sausages on the tips of their gleaming knives. At the dairy stalls, one farmer advertised the freshness of his eggs by tipping back his head, cracking an egg on his teeth and swallowing it raw. I shivered with admiration but shyly refused his invitation to try one.

The cheese stalls all smelled like sour milk, but the taste of the different types were as varied and full-bodied as the pink-cheeked, white-aproned fermieres who hacked away at the huge wheels as proudly as if they had made them themselves. Perhaps they had. There were always a few bits and crumbs that fell away from the wedge, and one special friend would scrape them up carefully on her knife, wink at Olga and ask, "Perhaps you have a mouse at home?" Olga never failed me. When I looked up at her hopefully she always answered, "I have the mouse with me." I would stretch out my brown mitten for the scraps. My mitten would smell of cheese, and the cheese would taste of wet wool, and both prolonged the pleasure.

On the way home we would stop at the patisserie just around the corner from our building. A bell tinkled as we went through the door and into a little room filled with the warm, yeasty smell of bread rising, the sweet smells of vanilla and chocolate, and the confitures of strawberry and black cherry. While Olga and Madame went through their ritual of discussing the weather, the health of each member of our family, and that of Madame's, I stood transfixed in front of the patisserie counter. Should I spend my centimes for a meringue that would melt like a cloud in my mouth, or for a great round Bun du Berlin, oozing dark jelly? The marzipan potatoes and pears were beautiful, but almond paste was not my favorite. Nor did I care for any cakes with rum flavoring. There were thin little leaf cookies covered with chocolate, brittle butterfly-shaped pastry cookies with a honey-colored glaze, and tartes aux apricots. I savored each one in anticipation until I was almost too glutted to make a decision. Usually it was a Bun du Berlin, because the outside was so crisp, the dough so tender, and the great pool of confiture within was a surfeit of delight.

Olga was a country girl, and with the first March thaw, her broad, peasant feet began to itch to "make a walk" to the mountain. She didn't mean Mont Blanc, which was of course *the* mountain. I saw it only a few times that winter. In the first place, you had to go to the other side of the lake and then look back, which we did every Sunday when we went to the American church. Perhaps there weren't many clear Sundays, but I do remember when I first saw Mont Blanc. I had run ahead of my mother and sister so that I could run down the cobbled ramp to the quay at the edge of the lake. I tossed the handful of crusts that I had brought for the muets, little mud ducks that swam along the shore of the lake, and then glanced up suddenly. There it was, a dream mountain, pure white, resting only on pale dove-grey clouds. And then, slowly, the clouds closed in front of it, and it was gone.

But Olga meant to "make a walk" to the nearest mountain, the Grand Salève or the Petit Salève. I can't remember which, and I have never seen the name written, so perhaps it is not spelled that way. I never doubted that Olga knew where we were going, and she never doubted it either. She always knew where she was going, but never how to get there. It didn't matter. Fortunately, I was born with some sort of internal compass that still tells me directions, so it is very hard for me to get lost. We packed our cheese, bread, and chocolate, and took a little train to the foot of the mountain. We climbed down out of the third-class compartment, and there was early spring. We could smell it in the damp ground steaming in the warm sunlight. We could smell it in the pussy willows, and as we clambered up the steep slopes we could smell it in the snowdrops, the wet mosses, and the milky, glacier-fed streams. We took off our sweaters and lay flat on the rocks. We threw snowballs at each other and rolled on the stiff warm grass. We came home exhausted and euphoric, arms full of pussy willows, my basket full of limp snowdrops, and the clear thin smell of spring in my clothes. Years later, in Vermont, when I watched the cows on their first day out in the meadow, bucking in awkward ecstasy, I have remembered that orgiastic welcome to spring.

Then spring came everywhere. The little church was filled with the heavy perfume of hyacinths. Old ladies in the caps of their various cantons sold bunches of violets on street corners, and the flower stalls at the market overflowed with the aroma of red-rimmed narcissi, drowning out the sour milk smell of the cheeses and the pungent strings of onions that wreathed the vegetable stalls.

It was May and there was a children's party. I don't remember who gave the party, or why, but there was a Maypole with stream-ers of pink and blue ribbons. Because I was the youngest, I was the May Queen. A wreath of pale yellow freesia was placed on my head, and I stood at the center of the Maypole while the others skipped and wove closer and closer to me. I felt beautiful and very important. I was Cinderella at the ball. I was a princess, and the sweet ethereal fragrance of freesia was a second halo around my head. I remember that there were meringues filled with whipped cream. I carried my crown home with me and hung it on the little ironwork balcony outside my window. I never threw it away. I don't know how long it stayed there, three stories above the narrow, steep street.

Not long after May Day I was told to pack my Swiss dolls in my wicker suitcase. Olga buttoned me into my travelling dress of navy blue pussy willow silk and Mother stuffed my collapsible fingers into white cotton gloves. A wide-brimmed, straw sailor hat was placed on my head and the white elastic snapped under my chin. We were going back to America, and spring in Geneva became my first, and recurrent, memory of the sixth sense of spring.

Valentine's Day

Old St. Valentine, the Roman martyr priest whose feast is on February 14, would be very much surprised to see what Hallmark, Whitman, and Russell Stover have done to his day. He did become the patron of love, but our current customs have less to do with him than with the coinciding Roman festival of Lupercalia, which celebrated the mating season of birds. Perhaps birds mate in February in Italy, but not in Vermont. The chickadees fluffed up at my feeder have only one thing on their minds, but it is food, not sex.

Most of our songbirds quite sensibly don't return north until their food becomes available. I always feel sorry for that early robin who is trying to pierce the frozen ground in a futile hunt for a worm in late March. All the bugs that annoy us in late spring, but are the supermarket for phoebes, swallows, and warblers, are certainly not available in February.

Lupercalia was celebrated by the exchanging of presents. Somehow the custom has survived almost two thousand years, perhaps because it was a welcome celebration of the first intimations of spring. Our great grandparents sent cards on which cupids, transfixed hearts, and bluebirds carried on the tradition.

When I was a child, Valentine's Day was a big deal in the lower grades. If we were lucky enough to have a heavy snowfall during the week before, a messenger from the principal's office (no intercoms then) would tell us that there would be no school that afternoon. Euphoria would prevail! We would rush home for lunch and spend the entire afternoon at home on the floor, attaching lace paper doilies onto red hearts with little folded paper hinges, and then embellishing them profusely with impaled hearts, cupids, violets, and roses. I can still smell the library paste. The floor would soon be littered with red and lacy scraps, and we would stick to everything we touched.

Funny cards had only begun to appear, and those professed loathing rather than love. The boys favored these but no one was fooled. If you got an insulting card, you knew it was from the boy who liked you. Half of the fun was in making these elaborate concoctions and planning who would be the recipients. The other half was the great day itself, when a big cracker box, the kind that bulk Saltines came in, was covered with red crepe paper, a slit was made in the top, and it was placed on the teacher's desk for us to stuff our creations into its depths. We were expected, with a little prodding from our mothers and teacher, to make a valentine for every child in the class. That was no problem. We had made so many that we had enough for our parents, grandparents, Sunday school teacher, and piano teacher. Then the moment came when we abandoned long division and the chief products of Brazil and sat nervously at our desks while two appointed tellers lifted off the crinkly lid, fished out the gaily-colored valentines, and went up and down the rows handing them out. We pored over them trying to figure out who "guess who?" might be. Do they still do that now? My daughter Debbie teaches third and fourth grade at the Flynn School and she says they do, but the valentines are bought, not made, and the Flintstones and comic book characters have replaced cupids and roses.

Of course, later on, when we were older, it was exciting to get a red heart-shaped box of chocolates on Valentine's Day. The box was treasured long after the chocolates were eaten, and became the repository for letters from the sender. Now that phone and fax have made letter writing a lost art, are love letters obsolete? It would be too bad if they are. But the volume of valentines in the card shop and big and little red satin boxes on the candy counters show that the Romans had a good idea.

Whether it is Asphodel in an alabaster urn, or a chocolate heart from Jericho's Snowflake Shop, it's still what Yogi Berra called "Déjà vu all over again."

ESCORT SERVICE

"Police Escort" conjures up an image of black stretch limousines with little foreign flags fluttering on the hoods. My own experience with a police escort has been more modest. In grade school we were escorted across Bloomfield Avenue by a large ruddy-faced Irish policeman we called Uncle Jim Mulligan. We called him that because he was the uncle of one of our classmates. He wore brown leather puttees with a yellow pencil stuck in the top of one of them, and a perpetual smile. He was always ready to admire a new bicycle or the horn-rimmed glasses I began to wear in the fourth grade.

After college, I maneuvered through the traffic of New York and Boston without the aid of a man in blue. In both cities they too were apt to be ruddy-faced Irishmen, with probably a good many Mulligans among them. Only once was I escorted by a policeman in New York. It was when I had to identify a burglar who had absconded with my pocketbook while posing as a steampipe-fitter in our new apartment. After a few minutes in court, my policeman offered me a ride back uptown. I assumed he meant a ride in his police car, but he meant a free ride on the subway with him (which cost a nickel at that time), after he told the lady in the booth that I was his prisoner! No handcuffs, but he did keep a firm grip on my arm until we got out of her sight.

Since then the police and I have travelled independently. They have responded to my urgent invitations when we have been robbed: once in Kansas and twice in Jericho. But after a few routine questions, they always left me to the dreary job of finding out exactly what had been stolen. George and I did have a police escort once in Switzerland. It was a rainy day and we couldn't find our hotel. A dapper gendarme hopped into his car and led us to the Novotel in Neuchatel.

But last fall I had a novel encounter with a police escort. The phone rang and a female voice identified herself as the dispatcher at the police barracks. She said a state trooper wanted to know where I lived.

"Why?" I countered.

"He has some people who want to find you."

"Who are they?"

"I'll ask him." There was a short delay while she talked to him on his radio.

"He doesn't know. They are in an out-of-state car behind him."

"Ask him if he is familiar with Jericho."

He told her he was and, assuming that anyone consulting the police was unlikely to be dangerous, I gave her the directions which she relayed to him. Then I waited with mounting curiosity. In fifteen minutes a police car drove in, followed by an RV with Ontario plates. The trooper waved and drove off, and three large senior citizens, a man and two women, dismounted from the RV.

I had never seen any of them before but they greeted me like a long lost friend. They turned out to be neighbors of an elderly lady, Elizabeth Hope, from Ayr, Ontario, who had read one of my books. When they were starting on a trip to Nova Scotia, Maine, and northern New England, they asked her if there was some souvenir she would like them to bring back for her from New England. Yes, she wanted them to go to Vermont and find that Marguerite Wolf who wrote the book, and take a picture of her and her waterfall. They accomplished both. It was clear that the police escort impressed them far more than the waterfall or I did. Canadian-American relations had reached a new all-time high.

NESTING PLACES

It always surprises me that birds are as diverse as humans in their choice of nesting sites, and share some of the same preferences we have. Some people thrive on the excitement of city life, elbowing through crowds on the street, and sleeping above, below, and next door to each other in apartments just like pigeons, English sparrows, and martins. Others dream of a homestead in Alaska, or of weaving a palm-frond shelter on a remote South Sea island. Kestrels and loons also seek out an isolated spot, as far away as possible from human interference. Most of my human and avian friends opt for the middle ground, the suburban life of neighbors within sight and sound. One spring, a phoebe completed her nest on a ledge of the porch in our old house before we put up the summer screens. You guessed it, we had to leave the screen door ajar until the fledglings left the nest, which pretty much defeated the function of the screens for several weeks.

For two years a female pigeon built her nest, a helter-skelter affair of a few sticks, in a rain gutter right below our bedroom window. When one of the violent spring thunderstorms sent a tidal bore of water rushing through the gutter, it washed out her nest and eggs. Pigeons are slow learners or creatures of habit, because she kept rebuilding the nest on the same site. It took three washouts before she reconsidered. I have friends who live on top of the San Andreas Fault in California. How many earthquakes does it take to scare off humans?

I wonder if some birds feel that their proximity to humans protects them from their natural wild predators. My neighbor, Clara Manor, has had house finches nesting in her hanging baskets of fuchsias, which presented a dilemma to Clara, not to the finch family. Should she water the fuchsia and risk chilling the eggs, or protect the birds and risk dehydrating the plant?

We have three bluebird houses and no bluebirds. Each year tree swallows nest in one that is at the edge of my path to the garden, but another one, farther out in the meadow, has never been occupied. The tree swallows dive bomb me when I walk past the bird house on the way to the garden. They never hit me, but I can feel the whoosh of their wings and hear the clicking noise they make to scare me off. Why don't they use the other nest, which is farther from the path? Or do they enjoy challenging my presence in their territory?

One spring, at the entrance of the Old Mill Craft Shop at Jericho Corners, cliff swallows built their grey cone-shaped mud nests, plastering them on a vertical wall under the eaves. Why did it stick, and why did they build it within reach of everyone going in and out of the shop? Obviously, like the pigeons and phoebes, they trusted the proximity of humans. I've read that swallows like to build near a wasp's nest. Presumably, the wasps don't bother swallows, but deter stingable predators.

I marvel at one Baltimore oriole's nest hung from the tip of an elm branch over a paved road. It has been there for three years, continuously pelted by ice, wind, snow, and rain storms. It's a tribute to the engineering skill of orioles, who weave a deep pouch of hair and string, line it with wool, and suspend it with grass and string from a crotch in a twig. They also like to build their nests over water. Does the wet pavement look like a stream?

We offered our geese a nesting box filled with straw. They preferred an old tire, however, which they lined with their own assortment of dried grass. It was just the right size for the female, round, like most nests, so that she could turn freely during her long vigil.

I've never found a hummingbird's nest, that walnut-size cup, lined with milkweed and thistle down, and shingled with bits of lichen. But other small nests I've admired are the tiny warblers' nests in gourds that Cathy Yandell has in her aviary. Such cozy little cabins! I can't see the inside of the nest, only the bright eyes of the tiny, brightly-colored inhabitants peering out of the hole.

Nesting is an atavistic urge. I know a travelling man who immediately sets out his family pictures and toilet articles, and puts away his extra clothing in the motel room drawers, even if he is staying only one night. A musician on tour told me that she takes a few small pillows, a special towel and soap, and books and pictures to make a little nest at each stop. Very few of us now live and die in the house in which we were born. Is it because our houses lack permanence that we are driven to accumulate so many things, toys, cars, and clothes as our lares and penates? I enjoy seeing new environments, but I don't like staying in motels or hotels. I feel as though I have no function, no role in those impersonal rooms. I am delighted to return home to sort through *my* mail, see what has happened in *my* garden, and do whatever small tasks need *my* attention. People used to have to carry coals from their old hearth to start the fire in their new shelter. We still do—not coals perhaps—but whatever is necessary to nurture the spirit, and to warm the hearth and heart in a new nest.

THE LISTERS

"Oh my God! I forgot my list!" The panic on this woman's face was met with sympathetic smiles as we wrenched our shopping carts out of their nested bondage at the supermarket.

The bereft lady turned abruptly and dashed back through the "out" automatic door, presumably to retrieve the vital list. So what, you say, if she forgot the poupon mustard, or the cold cereal that her grandson believed would assure him a physique like Arnold Schwarzenegger's? I'll tell you so what. After you have scurried up and down the aisles, juggled three huge bags of groceries, dropped your keys in a puddle, driven home and re-juggled the loot into the kitchen, it is not soothing to be met with "You forgot the 'Pec's Pumper'? Jeez! How could you forget THAT?"

I, too, am now a slave to a list. It wasn't always so. When my children were young, and were dashing off to school, the air was alive with the sound of "Will you take back my library book,

Mom?" and "Don't forget to pick up my pictures at the drug store," along with "Where did you put my lunch money?"

Did I jot down the many requests that came in daily? No, I just assumed I could remember them. Wrong. Out of ten items I would forget one, always the most important, the one without which life for that member of the family lost all meaning.

Now, when I only have my own errands to run and groceries to buy, I have a list near the door that I almost always remember to take with me to the store.

Grocery lists are not the only variety. I married a list junkie and my two daughters inherited his organizational genes. They need lists because they each live in a male-oriented household, with husbands and sons who take for granted the appearance of cooked food and matching socks.

One of the funniest lists I've seen in our family was when Debbie, about nine years old and annoyed with George for some reason, wrote on her blackboard, "People I like in this family: Patty and Mommy."

Now my daughters' lists include people to phone. In Patty's case MANY people to phone, to enlist in various school and community affairs. Debbie's lists include things to be taken to school, tickets to be bought, dentist's appointments, videos to be returned before the rental price goes up, and separate lists headed "Tell Mom" and "Ask Steve." Now that I too am addicted to lists, they clutter up my desk and table, but I am dependent on them to motivate my day.

One Sunday afternoon at Dave and Meredith Babbott's garden party, Dr. Jim Madison told me that he had proudly worked his way through most of his weekend list. In Jim's case, it probably involved hauling water from his pond to forty blueberry bushes, hoeing the garden, and mending or fixing all the parts of a house that routinely squawk for attention. When he told his wife, Joan, he was about finished, she said, "But you haven't seen *my* list!" The Madison's house, orchard, and garden always looks groomed and polished. Mine, especially now that I am alone, needs a list to propel me into action. George was the maintenance man, and he enjoyed doing everything himself, short of climbing onto the roof. Right up there with his companionship, I sorely miss his knack for fixing, repairing, or anticipating malfunctions. He was an insatiable lister, a long-term lister. On his list would be such items as "remodel the barn, clear out trees at the brook, review financial status." A list like that depresses me. My satisfaction comes from a sense of accomplishment as I cross off the completed items. Now that's fun! George didn't see it that way. He made fun of my lists, telling people that my lists included "Open eyes, get up, brush teeth, put sock on left foot, put sock on right foot, and eat breakfast." Now that's unfair! None of those items ever appeared on my list, though it would have given me pleasure to cross them off. I don't want a list so comprehensive that it hangs over me like a menacing storm cloud. If I can't cross off several items each day it is no fun at all. Attainable goals, that's what I like.

Maybe my sights are low, but when I cross off "do laundry, pick beans, write a piece about list addicts," I feel it is a day well spent.

THINGS THAT GO BUMP IN THE NIGHT

Why does life seem so difficult in the middle of the night? It's not just the dark. A problem at 9 p.m. is not nearly so ominous as the same problem at 3 a.m., when you wake with a sense of impending doom. It probably has something to do with your metabolic rate and your arterial blood supply. But the fact is, an unusual noise in the wee hours before dawn can make you sit bolt upright in bed and wonder why you opted to live alone in the country.

When you have a husband or children in residence you can at least share your anxiety, or in the case of your husband, perhaps the role of getting up and *doing* something about it.

Several years ago, there was a loud knocking on our front door at 1 a.m. George and I were sleeping upstairs because a visiting college friend was occupying the downstairs bedroom. The knocking was so imperative that George catapulted himself down our circular staircase so that the noise wouldn't waken our guest. He landed heavily, took two steps across the floor and fell, hit his head on the dining room table, and finally scrambled hastily to his feet. At the door was a teenage boy who wanted a ride up the road. He had no light on his bicycle and was having trouble staying on the road. George limped out to the garage, unaware that his face was bleeding and that he was wearing a short bathrobe. They put the bike in the back of the truck and started off up the road. When George asked where he lived, the boy said "A little farther, but let me off where the hardtop starts."

George got back to bed somehow, but the next morning he could not put his weight on that foot. A trip to the doctor confirmed his worst fears: a torn Achilles tendon, resulting in six weeks in a plaster cast, no driving, no golf, no swimming, no activity other than hobbling on crutches the whole summer.

We didn't know the boy, but we wondered why he didn't want to be taken to his house, and what he was doing out at 1 a.m. on his bicycle. We never saw him again, but his memory lingers on.

That was our most traumatic nocturnal episode, but there have been others since I've been alone that have been curiously alarming. A few weeks after George's death, I was awakened by the sound of the porch door being jiggled and thumped. It was a mild summer night, no wind. I listened with growing anxiety. Someone was fumbling with the door. With heart pounding, I crept to the front door, made sure it was bolted, and flicked on the porch light. A large raccoon was standing on his hind legs pushing against the screen door. He humped off into the woods, and I went back to bed with a foolish grin on my face.

Soon after, we had a power outage that lasted almost twenty-four hours. I coped in the daytime with the woodstove, and in the evening with candles and a flashlight. But it is always amazing to me how dependent we are on electricity. There is no water to flush the toilet or brush your teeth because our pump is activated by electricity. There is no cookstove, no TV, no typewriter, iron, or vacuum cleaner. We have a generator, but only George, Steve Page, and Bob Bechard know how to run it. I was settled more or less comfortably in bed when I heard a crash, followed by the sound of splintering glass somewhere in the house, which is not reassuring in total blackness. The intensity of the darkness at night with no garage light or night light is surprising. I grabbed a flashlight and forced myself to shine it all around the living room. Nothing. I went into the den and there on the floor was a frayed picture of our old house that had fallen off the wall, scattering glass everywhere. Why, after twenty years, did it choose to fall the night of the blackout?

One winter night I was awakened by the sound of someone shouting out on the road. I was afraid someone was hurt. I opened the bedroom window and could see the lights of a car, but the car itself was hidden by the barn. What I heard were cries for help, but not what I expected.

"Please don't turn away from me!" a man's voice shouted. He sounded desperate, on the verge of tears. "Please, please, don't turn away from me," he repeated over and over. I didn't hear any answering voice. Presumably the other person was in the car with the windows shut. I decided that the problem was a domestic one, not a physical injury, and really none of my business, so I shut the window. I heard the car drive away, and spent the next hour wondering who they were. Did she leave him stranded on the road? And why the unusual phrase?

I hear other voices in the night, but their owners usually come to the door, asking to use our phone after they have skidded off the road on the icy curve just beyond our house. The phone call is often to a parent, describing how bad the road was and how slowly he was going. But one night I heard a young woman's voice long before she reached the door.

"My husband will kill me! He'll kill me!" When I opened the door she said the same thing, not "May I use the phone?" just "He'll kill me. I know he'll kill me." She phoned the potential murderer and it was apparent that he didn't plan to kill her after all. He was relieved that she was unhurt. And when he turned up shortly and was able to rock the car out of the ditch, she finally stopped predicting her imminent demise.

At the end of March our road is a slough of despondency. Late one night, there was a rap on the door and a tearful voice croaked "Mrs. Wolf, please let me in." It was a friend of Debbie's, and she was very upset. Her car was on its side in the ditch (one of the new deep ditches they blasted out last summer to "improve" the drainage). She was unhurt. A man had offered her a ride, but that frightened her more so she had run to my house. During her long phone call to her husband, I kept suggesting that I have a neighbor pull her out. The message finally got through, and she let me call Cary Todriff, my idea of a knight in shining (red truck) armor. While we waited, four or five cars lurched by. Every single car stopped and asked if they could help.

"You certainly have nice neighbors," she remarked. But I didn't know any of them. Then Cary roared up with his smile and lights flashing, and had her car back on the road in no time. She offered to pay him and he just grinned. "Oh, that's all right. It was just around the corner."

"Let me live in a house by the side of the road and be a friend to Man" is a noble sentiment, but could I please have a turn on the daytime shift?

CAT TALES

Cats are mysterious creatures. That's probably why the Egyptians revered them. One look at Garfield and Odie will convince you that while Odie is a slavering, eager, loyal, but none-too-bright dog, Garfield regards both Odie and Jon, his human housemate, as inferior breeds who do not need to know and could not understand the intricate machinations of the cat's superior and devious mind.

Cats are neither loyal nor disloyal. They are opportunists. They know that their current human servant is the opener of cans and bags of cat food, and they tolerate strange and maudlin behavior because life runs smoother that way.

A dog loves you unconditionally, no matter how stupid you are. A cat accepts you, but clearly expresses disapproval if you go away or expect him to be gracious to your guests.

But how can this aloof and self-sufficient creature find his way home across the street or across the country? Mention this uncanny ability to a cat fancier, and you'll evoke another tale of the return of a displaced cat. If you can stand one more, I'll tell you what happened to me and a cat that wasn't even mine.

We had cats for years when we had a large barn full of animals, and most of our cats were barn cats. Now that I no longer harbor sheep, pigs, or chickens, and have a small carpeted house, I cannot have a barn cat, and I don't want a house cat. So when a small, adolescent, grey cat tried to adopt me, I resisted. She circled the porch, sat on a rock right outside the window, and scratched at the door. The message was clear, but I hardened my heart and did not feed her or let her in. I did phone around the neighborhood and posted a notice in Desso's store describing the cat. No one responded. I told my daughter and grandson who live ten miles away, and of course Morgan quickly volunteered to take on the cat. They put her in my Hav-a-hart trap and took her home to Williston. The cat lamented loudly during the ride, as is a cat's wont. The minute they got home Morgan opened the cage, and the cat shot out and took to the woods. In spite of looking and calling and rattling food dishes, the cat never darkened their door again.

Three days later, who should be once again grooming herself on the rock outside my window but the small grey cat, looking a little travel-weary, but ready to renew our one-sided relationship. I had never fed her, invited her in, or given her any reason to think of this house as a potential home.

On the verge of a trip to the animal shelter I confessed my dilemma to two cat-loving friends, Mary Wight and Helen Mann, both of whom offered to shelter the cat until we found it a home. Helen came out from South Burlington with a cat travelling case. I had invited the cat inside the screen porch, but when we tried to pick her up she bristled with fear and flew around the porch, climbing the screens. Helen deftly grabbed her, popped her into the case, and took her home, much to the disgust of her own resident cat. After she put an ad in the paper, she had eleven responses and gave the cat to the family that she considered real cat people. It was a compatible match and a happy ending, but that's not the point of this story.

What I want to know is how did that cat walk more than ten miles and cross the Winooski River? I doubt if it swam across that strong current. We once had a cat that swam with our children, but only short distances.

Mrs. Lynn Tracy of Evanston, Illinois, told me about their cat who liked to join them in their rowboat when they went fishing. It was a fastidious cat, and when nature called it jumped overboard, swam to shore, relieved itself, swam back, and climbed back into the boat. But that was on a calm lake. The Winooski River often floods and has eddies and a strong central current. There are two bridges in our area, one with heavy traffic at the junction of Routes 2 and 117, and the North Williston bridge, closed at that time to vehicular traffic, which would make it more attractive to a small homebound cat. That also would be the more direct route, if the homing instinct is governed by an internal compass responding to the earth's magnetic field. Studies on homing pigeons have shown that they have deposits of iron in their heads. Do cats? No one seems to know. I told you cats are mysterious. I can just picture Garfield's lowered eyelids and the caption reading, "Wouldn't you like to know?" Yes, I would. My curiosity was further whetted by a story Henry Frueh, pastor of the Williston Federated Church, told to the children one Sunday. When he was pastor of a church in Keeseville, New York, there was a widower in his congregation who had a cat named Snowball. His daughter was visiting him from Virginia, and he asked her if she would take Snowball home with her because he had to go on a trip. His daughter agreed, and she and Snowball returned to Virginia. After several weeks his daughter phoned to say that she had bad news. Snowball had disappeared. But two weeks later, her father in Keeseville heard a scratching on the kitchen door. There was Snowball, acting as though she had just been out for a morning stroll instead of an adventure of over eight hundred miles, fraught with unimaginable dangers and hardships. Those poor little paws! She must have used up most of her nine lives.

The Egyptians were right. We owe a little reverence to the mysterious powers of the cat, which we can't begin to understand.

Going Home

They say you can't go home again, that time enhances your memory, and that in the meantime both you and the place will have changed. I've found that to be true when you go back to a childhood home. Everything is smaller because you are bigger.

But last May I went back to a house that had been our home in the sixties. It is quite an unusual house. I wrote a chapter about it in *Vermont is Always With You.* The chapter was called "On Looking a Gift House in the Mouth," because this handsome Tudor mansion was given to the endowment association of the University of Kansas by Mr. and Mrs. Kenneth Spencer, to be used as the home of the Dean of the University of Kansas Medical College. When George became Dean, I automatically became chatelaine of a house that has eight bathrooms, bees in the walls, a Waterford chandelier and a ghost in the dining room, and an underground sprinkler system that is a smaller version of the fountains of Versailles.

We only lived there four years, and six other families have also lived there, two before and four after our time of stewardship. Last winter Jan Clawson, wife of the present Dean (now called Executive Vice-Chancellor), decided to write a booklet about the history of Spencer House and invited the families who had lived there in the past thirty-five years to a reunion at the time of the Medical College commencement. An invitation that includes round-trip air fare and hotel accommodations is hard for a Yankee like me to refuse—impossible, in fact. Besides, I was eager to see the house again as well as Mission Hills, one of the most beautiful residential areas in the country.

You know about the best laid plans. I presented myself at the Burlington airport and was promptly told that my plane had been cancelled. The only other flight available would get me to Kansas City at midnight; a hardship, I felt, for anyone meeting me. So I was rescheduled to leave the next day. Joan Cross had kindly come out from Burlington and took me to the airport, where she dropped me off and went on about her business. So there I was, all dressed up and nowhere to go, except to take a $25 taxi ride back home to Jericho.

Chad Burnell, who mows my lawn, was surprised to see me pull up in a taxi. So was Joan when I phoned and asked her to guess where I was. Chad rose to the occasion and offered to take me to the airport the next day, and in the waiting room at the airport there was Joan! She had come to make sure that I was actually airborne this time. I was, and flew into the new (for me) airport which is way out in the fields of Missouri. When we lived in Kansas the airport was right downtown, ten minutes from our house. Standing at the gate was a chauffeur holding a large sign that asked "ARE YOU MAGGIE WOLF?" I was whisked off in a limousine to the senior luncheon at the Medical Center. When George was Dean, we invited the seniors and their parents to brunch at Spencer House, where they sat at tables on the lawn. But I was deposited at the courtyard of the Medical Center where tents had been set up and a huge crowd was milling around. "That looks like a lot of people," I commented to the departing chauffeur. "About fifteen hundred," he said.

There I was, clutching my little suitcase and raincoat at the edge of fifteen hundred people, and not a familiar face in sight. I decided that inasmuch as I was the only foreign body with a suitcase, someone would identify me. Someone did. Dr. Clawson, the Vice Chancellor, came up, introduced himself, pinned a gardenia corsage and name tag on me, and led me to Dr. Bob Hudson, who had been at KU when we were there. Bob gave me a tour of the famous Clendenning Library and the Chancellor's corridor, where I saw George's portrait for the first time. It had been painted in Vermont by Stan Marc Wright and shipped to KU as soon as it was finished. I have a picture of it, but had never seen the original.

After lunch, Dr. Clawson took me to the hotel at the Crown Center, the one where a balcony in the enormous foyer collapsed a few years ago, killing a great number of people. The balcony had been rebuilt, and I walked on it. It didn't collapse, but the management would rather you didn't remind them of the tragedy.

In my spacious room on the twenty-second floor was a bowl of fruit, a cheese tray, and a bottle of wine. In the adjoining room were my old friends Clarke and Barbara Wescoe, and we had a great private reunion. We had lived in the same apartment building in New York City in the forties, where our first children were born. It was across the street from New York Hospital, where George and Clarke were on the house staff. Clarke had gone on to become Dean, and then Chancellor of KU. George had been Dean of the University of Vermont College of Medicine, and then was at Tufts when Clarke lured him to KU.

Clarke and Barbara and I drove out to Spencer House and were delighted to find the house and gardens more beautiful than ever, and the interior greatly improved. The rather dark, sunken living room was now carpeted and furnished in soft pastel shades, the sunporch was now a cozy sitting room, and the den has become a very elegant study.

The Clawsons took me on a tour of Mission Hills. When we lived there, Mrs. Russell Stover lived right across Mission Drive and swam daily in her saltwater pool. Ewing Kauffman, owner of the Kansas City Royals, lived down the street in an Italianate fortress. He still does. It has fifteen bathrooms, a golf driving range in the basement, a pipe organ, and a library with a goldleaf ceiling. Things were not only up-to-date in Kansas City, everything was done on a large scale. In May, with redbud, forsythia, and every kind of flowering crab tree, the whole area was in bloom. My visit convinced me that you can go home again and find it as exciting as the first time you stepped over the threshold into a new life.

COUNTING
YOUR CHICKENS

My chickens are gone now, and I miss them. We had laying hens in the barn for twenty years after we came back to Vermont to live year round. In the fifties, when we wintered in South Burlington and summered here in Jericho, we had day-old chicks, ducks, turkeys, and a little South American hen who laid blue eggs. That's more years spent in poultry raising than I spent tending my children.

Is it the chickens I miss, or could it be having something living dependent on me? For years I looked forward to the day when I wouldn't have to think about someone else, free to come and go when and where I pleased, no alarm clock to shut off, no finding that lost mitten before the school bus lumbered around the corner.

I don't miss the alarm clock. I don't miss hunting for all the lost articles every member of the family believed I purloined. "What did YOU do with my history paper, my bank statement, my library book?" Now I am responsible for only my own lares and penates, and suddenly I am asking myself "What did you do with that last interest check?" I refuse to blame it on aging. It is simply that I am less attentive when I have less to attend to.

I was never naive enough to think that the chickens cared about me. There is probably no animal less caring than a chicken. If one of the flock dies, the rest of them don't even bother to step around it. They step on it. Their enthusiastic rush to the door when I arrive was only a conditioned response to the orts container in my hand. You don't know what "orts" are? Then you don't do crossword puzzles. Every week some puzzle will ask for "treat for Fido" or "table scraps" or "kitchen leftovers." That's what orts are. The dictionary says "bit, end, tag, morsel, and scrap." Chickens eat their mash and scratch in a desultory manner, but they become ecstatic and orgiastic over orts. You may feel the same way about truffles or Glenlivet scotch.

They didn't love me and I didn't love them, but I liked them. I could never bring myself to lop off their heads, but I felt no remorse when George did it. I dunked them in hot water, pulled off their soggy feathers, and eviscerated them with no sadness, just a lot of distaste for that aspect of animal husbandry.

But I miss them. I gave away the last nine old girls because I didn't think I should skid down the icy path to the barn twice a day in winter while living alone. If I fell and couldn't get up in sub-zero weather, I would freeze to death. They say it's a nice way to go, but if so, why don't suicidal types choose the ice floe or snowbank? I have to be sensible now that I have reached the age of osteoporosis, and limit my risks. I don't miss cleaning the chicken coop or struggling with 100-pound grain bags. I do miss finding those large brown eggs in the nests. I miss the murmuring of sleepy hens and their silly way of squatting when they are in your way. I miss their companionable clucking, but most of all I miss the feeling of having animals on a place that was once a farm. I think animals should serve a useful purpose. Our chickens weren't pets. Neither were the pigs or the sheep. Their lives were devoted to the production of food and my role was to supply the housing and nourishment they required. It was a mutually dependent relationship.

Part of my pleasure in a vegetable garden is similar. To nurture living plants that eventually nurture you is a symbiotic relationship lacking in urban life. I can't go back into the egg business, or loading pigs or raising children, and I wouldn't want to. Long ago I gave up pondering the old question, "Which came first, the chicken or the egg?" I'm just very glad my life included many years of pleasure from them both.

BUG OFF

Part of the fun of a vegetable garden is that each growing season is different. One year the cool-loving plants, like peas, lettuce, and spinach, will flourish, but the beans will develop fungi. The next year the peas will be jaundiced, and the warm weather crops, like peppers, beans, tomatoes, and corn, will bask in the heat of the sun.

Every trip to the garden brings a new miracle or disaster. The zucchini will have suddenly burst into extravagant golden blossoms, or the Colorado beetles will have appeared overnight on the potatoes and will need to be hand picked and stepped on, or, if you are squeamish, dropped into a jar of kerosene.

The battle of the bugs can be an ongoing conflict. All members of the cabbage family are host to those nasty little green worms, and striped beetles may have discovered the cucumbers.

But this year, for reasons which I can take no credit, our garden has been a bugless wonder. For the first time in over forty years of planting vegetables, not one potato bug has appeared. No, that's not quite true. One turned up on an eggplant, which belongs to the same solanum family, but he was obviously a sterile orphan. There have been no cucumber beetles, no squash borers, no cabbage worms. In fact, my pesticide Sevin is languishing on the shelf, unused. True, I planted radishes among the squash and nasturtiums, and marigolds with the beans, but I had done that for the last five years without achieving a bugfree garden.

The garden is fenced, so rabbits have never been a problem, but almost every year a woodchuck burrows under the fence at some point and feasts on broccoli heads or beans. I didn't plant corn this year for the first time because growing it for the raccoons doesn't seem cost effective in terms of time and frustration. We've tried many deterrents: planting pumpkins with the corn, using red pepper or moth balls, and stringing an electric wire around the top of the fence in August. But the raccoons have usually managed to find a way to get the corn the night before we planned to pick it.

This year has been different in all respects. No bugs, no raccoons, no woodchucks, not even a vole. I haven't even seen my old friend, a grandfather toad, who was beneficial. Early in June I was horrified to find deer prints in the soft earth of the garden. Nothing seemed to have been eaten. The young lettuce and pea vines were intact. But what could I do to discourage a deer? He could sail over our fence with the greatest of ease. I saw one do it one winter day, and watched him paw the earth for frozen carrots and beets. But we've never had one in the garden during the growing season. I shook some animal repellent that smelled like moth balls, only more so, around the garden, but didn't put much faith in it because the box had been in the garage for at least ten years.

Then one day I came home and found that our smoke alarm was making that insistent tick-tick sound it makes when the battery is in extremis. I pulled it out of the wall, but it went on ticking. The sound drove me crazy so I put it in the garage, planning to get a new battery. That night, one of those light bulbs flashed in my head like they do in the comic strips. If gardeners are urged to put a radio in the garden to discourage wildlife, why not my ticking smoke alarm? I hung it in a plastic bag on a garden fence post, hoping it might discourage the deer. I expected it would stop in a night or two. That was the first week in June. It is now the end of August, and it is still ticking at ten second intervals, a real high-pitched "peek peek" that I can hear from the house. Maybe it wasn't terminally ill after all. Maybe the deer has found other browse. But just maybe, O happy thought, I have discovered a new method of keeping our wildlife on the public side of the fence.

MY UNWELCOME MAT

We have an imprinted doormat, but it doesn't say "Welcome." It says "Go Away." It really does, in big black letters. Patty gave it to George for his birthday only a few weeks before he died, to make him smile. He loved it and wanted me to keep it there. I have, but no one takes the message to heart. Maybe because most of the time I don't want them to.

I don't expect my friends and family to pay any attention to it. In fact, I don't really want anyone who is already on my doorstep to feel that I am anti-social. But a few times a year, someone who has read my books becomes curious enough about me to find her way up our back road, book and camera in hand, to try to meet the lady who writes books.

What they see must be a disappointment. I am invariably just up from the garden, in muddy boots and an assortment of clothes that have seen better years. Sometimes I get a warning. Once it was a phone call from our general store. Lil Desso had the kindness to alert me that the occupants of a station wagon with Mississippi plates just asked how to find my house. But Desso's is only two miles away, hardly enough time to turn a sow's ear into a silk purse. In they came, five ladies in stretch pants that had to do just that. They had a written list of questions about my health, welfare, and pursuit of happiness. They wanted me to pose for a group picture with my arms around as many as I could reach, and inscribe loving messages in their books. I had never seen them before in my life. It was a one-sided relationship; they felt they knew me from my books, and forgot that I didn't know them at all.

Sometimes it works out to my advantage. An attractive young couple who had driven all the way from Texas, not just to see me of course, but to explore New England, turned out to be a real addition to my life. I enjoyed their visit and after they returned to Texas, they sent me a wonderful book of essays about backcountry Texas people, a world apart from Houston or Dallas. When my new book came out, I sent them a copy to try to even up the score, but was completely surprised when they sent me a sweatshirt hand-painted with bluebonnets. The next year on Valentine's Day, they sent me a sweatshirt with the inscription "Someone in Texas loves you." I wear it often and think of them fondly.

I tolerate the small Girl Scouts and the large firemen because our girls once sold Girl Scout cookies, and there's always the possibility that I might need the services of our volunteer firemen one day, but I consider salespersons and Jehovah's Witnesses an invasion of privacy. They make me feel guilty if I turn them away, and miserable if I listen. The spring when George was very sick, a carload of Jehovah's Witnesses parked in the driveway. They always bring a child or two, which I think is devious because they know that you will be reluctant to be rude in front of the children.

On this occasion I had no intention of letting them in. So I simply said "I'm sorry. My husband is dying." As soon as the words were out of my mouth I was afraid they would want to rush in and pray. But this time, the first in my experience, they were speechless, frozen in their tracks for a second, and then they turned and fled back to their car, tumbling over each other in their eagerness to escape. With one door still open they roared out of the driveway. I felt no remorse. It was the truth and the truth had set me free!

READY, WILLING, BUT NOT QUITE SO ABLE?

"Old gardeners never die, they just spade away," Muriel Cox once said. That may be true, but I'm learning that they spade at a different tempo. I can remember when I could put in the whole garden, sixty by eighty feet, in one day. Not anymore. Actually I don't have to do any spading. Bob Bechard rototills the garden, but after I have raked out a portion of Vermont's perennial stone crop and planted a few rows I am ready to resume a vertical position and creak back up to the house.

Getting down on my knees is easy, but I don't just bounce back up like a Jack-in-the-Box anymore. I have to push up with at least one hand, unless there is something handy to pull on. I don't consider myself decrepit, though. In spite of statistics, I don't even consider myself old, but there is a noticeable difference in my agility.

If I refuse to give up gardening, and I certainly do, what can be done about my limited energy? Well, I've found a few conservation aids. Compost and mulch of every kind, straw, black plastic, and newspapers cut down on the weeding. The latest information on using newspapers is that you can use the comics and colored pages safely because the lead content in the ink is lower than it formerly was. They're not sure about those glossy inserts, so it's better to not use them until more tests have been run. Wide rows help too. I plant carrots, beets, onions, and all the cabbage family in blocks now, so there are fewer aisles for the weeds. You can set seed potatoes in thick mulch and let the potato plants grow up through it. The roots poke down into the earth, but the tubers grow right in the mulch, which keeps them immune to scab or soil-borne diseases. I have to admit I haven't tried it yet because I am not convinced that I wouldn't get more greened areas on the tops of the tubers. Why not plant pole beans and tall peas that can be picked standing up? You can't beat Kentucky wonders, Telephone peas, or Alderman peas for flavor, and Sugar Snap peas produce their pods at eye level.

Even more sensible is planting the vegetables that your family likes best. We love peas, and they freeze better than any other vegetable. We like beans, but not frozen, so we eat them every day for two months and can couple of loads. There is really no need for us to supply the whole county with zucchini, when most of our neighbors are trying to unload their surplus on us. This year I showed great self control and planted only one hill, along with several of Peter Pan, which everyone, including the neighbors, liked better anyway. Fresh broccoli at the supermarket in the winter is better than frozen, so we cut back on the number of plants. Onions are easy to grow and we just let them dry, put them in onion bags, and hang them in a cool place, where they last until the next year's crop are greentails. I haven't bought an onion in years. Two pounds of sets will do it.

Weeds in the asparagus used to be a problem, but a heavy mulch of our chicken litter (manure and shavings) keeps them down. I mulch them well before they emerge in the spring, and again in the fall. There used to be talk of using salt to keep down the weeds in asparagus. The horticulturists at the College of Agriculture at the University of Vermont say that salt doesn't do asparagus any good. That myth arose because asparagus can tolerate salt better than many plants. Kipling wrote:

Oh Adam was a gardener,
And God, who made him, sees
That half a proper gardener's work
Is done upon his knees.

He probably never had those knee pads that strap onto your knees. I think they're uncomfortable. I've got a handsome knee cushion with rubber on the back that a friend brought me from England. It's so pretty I hate to get it muddy. Actually, my problem is not sore knees. It's the upping and downing. I'd like one of those kneeler's pads that has sturdy steel handles to help you up. I see lots of women, older than I, bending over stiff-kneed, weeding or picking. It may be easier on the knees, but it's hard on the back, and not recommended by the orthopedists. If you plant less, hoe less, and fret less about a weedfree garden, there is no age limit, as Scott Nearing proved in his nineties. Thomas Jefferson was past eighty when he wrote "I'm still devoted to the garden...although an old man, I am but a young gardener."

An hour in the garden will limber your spirits as well as your joints. Anxiety about the health and welfare of children and grandchildren will evaporate with the morning dew. Ponce de Leon should have searched no farther than his patio.

OUT OF THE BLUE

If you think "cats and dogs" is an ancient description of precipitation, you are quite right. In Northern mythology, the cat is supposed to have great influence on the weather, and the dog, as a symbol of wind, was an attendant of Odin, the storm god. Even earlier, manna was miraculously supplied to the Israelites on their journey through wilderness from Egypt to the holy land, though that seems to have been an isolated windfall. Chicken Little caused quite a lot of consternation in the barnyard by announcing that the sky was falling, but that turned out to be a false alarm. And then there has been the occasional meteorite hurtling down out of the wild blue yonder and finding its final resting place in the Museum of Natural History in New York.

But now what do you think is falling in Maine? Trout. The Department of Inland Fisheries is restocking lakes by dropping trout from airplanes. Now some of those lakes are pretty small, and the pilot would have to be very accurate not to accidentally bean an unsuspecting tourist or fisherman. Have you ever been hit on the head by a falling chestnut or an apple? You know what gravity can do. A trout weighing about a pound would gain a lot of speed in its two-hundred-foot fall. Being felled by a fish is no laughing matter. Maybe you had better pack your motorcycle helmet along with your L.L. Bean waders.

If you have any doubt about the stupidity of the human race, something which seems to increase in proportion to its involvement with the military, let me tell you what was dreamed up back in 1941. A dental surgeon in Pennsylvania (and you know what sadists they can be) was so upset about Pearl Harbor that he wanted to attach incendiary bombs to bats and drop them over Japan. Do you think they had a good laugh over that in the Pentagon before they tossed it into the paper shredder? No indeed. Laughter does not come easily to the Kamikaze mind. They began to research what kind of bat would be suitable. It took them two years to choose the free-tailed bat, that could "fly fairly well with a one ounce bomb." Thousands of bats were refrigerated to induce hibernation so they could be attached to the dummy bombs. Then they were dropped from a B-25 bomber flying at five thousand feet. What happened, you eagerly ask? SPLAT! Most of the bats were still too sleepy to fly, and died on impact. So the army, in its infinite generosity, offered the idea to the navy, who leased four caves in Texas and assigned marines to guard them. A year later the project was cancelled because the Pentagon was running out of branches of the military on which to unload stupid ideas.

No wonder convertibles have gone out of style. Maybe the only safe form of precipitation is mercy, which, according to Portia, "droppeth as the gentle rain from heaven." It's a beautiful speech, but Shakespeare hadn't heard of acid rain.

THESE ARE A FEW OF MY FAVORITE THINGS

Much as I like the songs from "The Sound of Music," girls in white dresses with blue satin sashes are not my favorite things. The favorite things that would pull me back to Vermont, if I had the misfortune to be temporarily exiled, are seasonal events, which embody a unique combination of excellence and simplicity.

One of these events happens each September in villages throughout the state: the annual chicken pie supper. It is a feast of comfort food, snowy mountains of mashed potatoes and golden squash, featherlight biscuits blanketing savory chicken and gravy. No peas, no carrots, no celery, just generous bites of chicken in rich gravy, followed by wedges of apple or pumpkin pie. It is a fundraiser that raises more than money. It raises the spirits of teenagers trying not to show they enjoy it, and grandparents who are proud that they are.

A large segment of the community cooks, serves, washes dishes, or just comes to eat and talk with neighbors they may only pass on the road during the rest of the year.

Another favorite thing is the Vermont Symphony's Fourth of July concert at Shelburne Farms, something rapidly becoming traditional for many families. It too is multigenerational. Extended families bring their picnics, set up their folding chairs, spread their blankets, and unload their baskets. No chicken pie here, but the picnics range from the one next to us complete with champagne, candelabra and flowers, to baby bottles and peanut butter and jelly sandwiches. In recent years our delegation has included our two daughters and their husbands, my son-in-law's father, Russel Page, the three grandsons, and me. Three generations, who in spite of the vocal protests of the teenage grandsons, had a great time together. Our blanket was spread with marinated shrimp, barbecued chicken, crudites, french bread, white wine, cheese and fruit—very chic but very simple.

The sunset was reflected in the lake as we sat back together to enjoy the music. The reluctant boys were delighted to find that the Vermont National Guard had supplied real cannon and soldiers for the finale of the 1812 Overture, and as the sky darkened, fountains of multicolored fireworks erupted overhead, greeted by the predictable "oohs" and "ahhs" of the audience. As we folded our blanket and chairs and rounded up the boys, a peach-colored moon rose over Camel's Hump as a benediction to another memorable event.

One of the simplest, and best, of my favorite things is the band concert in Williston. Williston's bandstand is surrounded by wide lawns. The band is composed of local musicians, some professional, some amateur, but all dedicated, who gather several Wednesday evenings in the summer for an almost impromptu concert. As they cacophonously tune up, the audience trickles in with folding chairs or blankets, and settles here and there on the grass. The repertoire is a mixture of classical and popular music, songs from operettas, and marches. The moment that the band strikes up, all the small children shed their parental apron strings to join the other children and march, skip, or gallop around and around the bandstand. Tiny toddlers stagger after the nimble eight-year-olds, who make the circuit three times to one of the little fellows. In contrast to the audience of two thousand at Shelburne Farms, the scattered clusters of listeners may only add up to a hundred, but the applause is lively.

It is obvious that the members of the band are having a fine time. When a summer visitor band member sings the "Teddy Bear Picnic" with realistic growls, everybody laughs. Between the selections, the laughter of the musicians over some inside joke is so contagious that the audience laughs, even though they have no idea what is so funny. Terry Carpenter leads the band with musical skill and the expertise of twenty years experience in conducting. The concert is simple, beautiful, and moving. And when the final number, "Star-Spangled Banner," is played, the audience stands and sings while a jet plane swims across the darkening sky, blinking almost in time with the music. I am blinking too, happy to be alive, to be in Vermont, surrounded by a caring community.

LOVABLE LLAMAS

Llamas in Vermont? Are you kidding? Vermont is the land of milk and honey or, to be more accurate, of milk and maple syrup. Of course we have honey too, and value our bees and pollinators for our apple crop, but maple and cheese products usually get top billing as tourist attractions.

Can you picture Ethan Allen leading a llama up the trails on the Green Mountains, or Calvin Coolidge posing beside a llama in a Peruvian llama wool cap?

Llamas have been domesticated in the Andes for over a thousand years, and now have been brought into our hemisphere, where they are thriving from Oregon to Alabama, and many states in between. There still are many more in Bolivia and Chile than in the United States, but the gap in llama population is narrowing rapidly. The International Llama Convention, held in Burlington June 25–29, 1992 at the Sheraton Conference Center, drew 768 people, 120 llamas, twenty alpacas, and a lot of attention. It also drew a crowd of two thousand spectators to watch the llama parade in downtown Burlington. Of course not all the llamas in the parade were native Vermonters. Neither were their owners, but there are now thirty-two owners in Vermont and three hundred llamas.

My neighbors, June and Howard Taylor, have had two llamas for several years, and their attitude towards the gentle creatures is almost parental. June took a week off from work to help organize the convention. Their llamas were not in the parade because they are not used to public appearances, and their llamamama was busy hosting the visitors.

My daughter Debbie had agreed to help June, and I told Debbie I would be glad to be useful too. I pictured myself signing in registrants or handing out literature. Never in my wildest fantasies did I envision myself as a pooper-scooper, bringing up the rear of a llama parade! But armed with a scooper, dustpan and plastic bags, I found myself marching between Debbie, who wore a soulful deadpan Halloween mask, and an unknown girl completely concealed by a cow costume. I'm not sure of the significance of the cow costume, but Vermont never loses an opportunity to advertise its chief product. But there we were, part of a colorful parade of groomed and bedecked llamas and alpacas marching through the main streets of downtown Burlington between crowds of onlookers.

The purpose of our roles was not so much sanitation as education, to initiate the viewers into the benefits of llama manure. In each small plastic bag of manure we handed out was a slip of paper describing the virtues of the product, its lack of odor (it smells like earth), its high nitrogen potency, and its ease of handling (it is dry pellets). Oddly enough, the fastidious llamas, who have discreet private habits, were not eager to share their by-product at the beginning of the parade. They minced along daintily, batting their long eyelashes, twitching their furry, horn-shaped ears, regarding the people with interest, but showing no inclination to relieve themselves in public. I began to think that Debbie and I were there only for comic relief at the end of a dignified parade. Some of the llamas wore brightly colored ear tassels that are used for identification in South America. Some pulled little carts or wore saddle bags, showing their usefulness as beasts of burden. Their owners, who were leading them along, wore a variety of costumes including hats made out of llama wool. The alpaca wool trade is of major importance in Bolivia. It is as soft as cashmere and equally expensive.

Not everything about llamas and alpacas is expensive. Although a top female recently sold for $30,000, the average is $3,000 to $7,000. One male in Red Deer, Alberta, sold for $78,000, but usually a female commands a higher price. A breeding fee can run from $300 to $3,000. But the upkeep is cheaper than that of a large dog or horse.

Llamas are camelids. The small vicuna was the original one in Peru, and there are still wild guanacos in Patagonia. The largest concentration is now in Bolivia. Machu Pichu, the lost city of the Incas, was dependent on llamas and alpacas for all transportation of goods. But the Spanish wiped out the Incas and great numbers of their domesticated camelids. Fortunately, enough of the wild animals survived because they are perfectly suited to the climate of the Andes. They seem to like it here in Vermont too, and the International Llama Convention was a great exposure for these animals that many Vermonters have seen only in a zoo.

When the onlookers at the parade had satisfied themselves that the llamas would not bite, scratch, or kick, they began to pat and fondle them as though they were stuffed toys. As they closed in on them the shy beasts lost their inhibitions and soon a rain of pellets sent us scurrying to scoop the black gold into our plastic bags. The reaction of the public on being presented with a bag of llama manure was gratifying. No one refused the gift. Everyone smiled and thanked us and accepted our small offerings with grace and enthusiasm. Can you imagine their reaction if we had tried the same thing with sheep or cow droppings? It all goes to show you that Vermonters regard the llama as someone "from away," with mystical attributes. Our everyday local product from cows or sheep, even if sundried, would have been too familiar.

Never underestimate the selling power of a dainty, graceful creature with a velvety nose, long silky eyelashes, and a wistful expression!

LIKE A BAT
OUT OF HELL

"You can help us count bats," was the way I was greeted by
Ruth and Larry Van Benthuysen when I arrived to spend the night
at their house in Wells River.

Hardly an expert on the flying mammals, my only experience
with bats had been one summer many years ago when we rented
a converted barn in Underhill. My dismay when the bats began
soaring around the rafters the first night turned into admiration
when I realized that they kept our unscreened barn virtually in-
sect-free. But when I had to get up at night to fix baby Debbie a
bottle, I fervently hoped that the bats would maintain their alti-
tude well above my head.

Why were the Van Benthuysens offering a bat count as the
evening's entertainment? They had been remodeling an older home
in this northeastern Vermont town, and one of the dubious trea-

sures they found in their attic was an accumulation of bat guano. As conservationists they are all for bats as a natural form of insect control. But when their next door neighbors reported seeing over a hundred bats come out of their house at dusk, they embarked on intensive bat research and investigated methods of bat control.

Their quest led them to a book, *America's Neighborhood Bats* by pathologist John Rice, and advice on evicting their resident bats. Ladders were propped up against the roof, and netting was attached all around the chimney and the metal flashing, under which the bats flew out each evening. The netting was fastened down all around with duct tape except on the bottom, where it was left loose. The theory was that the bats, when they emerge for their nightly foraging, would slide down and out under the loose part of the netting, but be unable to get back up under it at dawn.

So precisely at 8:25 in the evening, we paraded across the lawn carrying our folding chairs as though we were going to a village band concert. Nothing happened for a few minutes, and I began to make snide remarks about fantasies and fallacies of vampires.

"There's one," Ruth shouted, and far up on the roof, a small black knob the size of a mouse emerged from under the flashing, skidded under the loose netting, spread its surprisingly wide wings, and swooped off.

"Two!" we shouted in unison. "Three, four. There's one caught at the side." Several more were confused by the netting and explored the fastened-down sides before they found the escape hatch. "Five, six, seven." The count accelerated for the next twenty minutes, and the air was full of flying bats.

Care to guess how many bats we counted? Ninety-five! Now, unless you are a bat fancier, that's more bats than most of us want to shelter under our roofs.

We folded up our chairs and went back indoors. A few minutes later, a bat swooped through the living room, passing by our heads expertly, but close enough to feel the swish of air from its wings. Bats in the belfry are one thing, but Larry and Ruth didn't welcome them in their living quarters, so Larry promptly turned on all the lights and the bat retreated into the back hall and out the door, hastily opened by Larry.

I can take bats or leave them alone, and until that evening I've left them alone. I am not especially afraid of bats, but I must admit that I closed my bedroom door that night and shoved a woven rug across the crack at the bottom.

Did the netting work? I went home the next day, but overcome by curiosity, I phoned Larry the next night. It took a long time before he answered the phone. He was, of course, outside on the neighbor's porch counting bats. How many? Twenty-three that night, which was a distinct improvement over the night before, but it didn't account for how those twenty-three got back in. Or did they sleep in that night?

And what has happened since? A SASE to the Van B's produced the following tally: thirteen the following night, ten the next, fourteen the next. A week later they were down to one, and in Larry's words, "thinking bat-free thoughts."

Of course, they realize that all those bats are alive and well somewhere in Wells River, swooping around each night, emitting their ultrasound squeaks fifty times a second and navigating by echolocation. They are sonar experts. When we walked across the lawn that first night, the bats were all around us, but no nearer than a rush of air.

The Van B's are grateful for their insect control. As a public relations man, Larry is aware that bats have suffered from misinformed and damaging press. But times are changing. No sooner had I come home than my neighbor showed me a bat house he had just finished. Bluebird houses are no longer *de riguer*. The ultimate in ambience is a bat house mounted near your gazebo. In Ireland, the value of a house for sale is increased if you claim there are bats in the attic. The next week I heard Rich Chipman, a wildlife biologist with the Department of Agriculture and graduate student at the University of Vermont, speak on "Bats in Your Belfry" at the Aiken Center.

Cheer up chiroptera! Even if we can't hear your ultrasound squeaks and rarely see your take-offs, we appreciate your exterminating ability. One bat can eat up to two thousand bugs a night. I don't know how many night-flying insects you have in your yard, but that is deluxe pest control. There is another plus. Bat guano is a hot item commercially. You are not likely to have enough in your attic to go into business, but 100,000 tons were mined from a cave in the southwestern United States. Another plus is that while our Vermont bats are insectivorous, there are bats in the tropics that feed on fruits and flowers. In fact bananas, avocados, guavas, and other plants are dependent on them for fertilization. And if Tequila is in your liquor cabinet, you can thank the bat for pollinating the Mexican agave, or century plant.

Are you still prejudiced because of age-old myths? The most prevalent one is completely false. Bats do not get caught in your hair. Their sonar system is more sophisticated than anything that man has dreamed up. Neither are our Vermont bats vampires. Only a few species, none of them in North America, feed on the blood of large sleeping mammals.

What about "as blind as a bat?" No, they are not blind, but their echolocation and ears are so much more effective than their eyes that their eyes seem to be useless.

Granted, the bat is not as cuddly as a Koala or a Teddy bear, but he's much more useful. Maybe we ought to sweep these myths out of the attics of our minds, and welcome the bats in our belfry.

"DWELL IN THE MIDST OF ALARMS"

— *William Cowper*

Alarms have always invaded our lives. I remember that the clanging of the elementary school tardy bell struck terror to my small heart if I was still on the playground instead of in my classroom seat, the kind that was attached to the desk which had an inkwell and numerous scratched initials.

I loved the excitement of town fire alarms as a child. We would jump on our one-speed bicycles and pedal off to the conflagration if it was anywhere in our neighborhood. You knew the approximate location of the fire by the number of the blasts of the Klaxon at the fire station in Montclair, New Jersey. It was so loud that if it blew when I was near the firehouse I let go the handle bars and put my fingers in my ears, with predictable bruising results.

But burglar alarms didn't come into my life until I was middle-aged. I remember being on Fifth Avenue when a store burglar alarm went off, causing all the passers-by to gather around staring into the plate glass window.

It didn't occur to us to have a home security system when we lived in Ardsley, New York, Weston, Massachusetts, or Mission Hills, Kansas. In fact, in our old house in South Burlington, Vermont, we had to hunt for the old-fashioned key to give to Helen Tilley if we were going to be away for a few days. That house was always unlocked and ironically it was the only one of our homes that was never robbed. Don't misunderstand. I'm not advocating leaving a house unlocked. I am just guessing that South Burlington in the fifties and sixties was more open and safer. We would have thought that anyone with a security system was paranoid. At that time, security systems were commercial rather than residential, and came in the form of sleek Dobermans, who roamed the aisles of Macy's at night, or a drowsy night watchman, flatfooting through a shopping area on his regular beat.

But after our second robbery in Jericho in the seventies, in the daytime when the house was securely locked, George got uneasy. The first time he had come home to find the phone wire cut, the house ransacked, and one casement window hanging askew. His guns, a fancy radio, my father's gold pocket watch, and my mother's engagement diamond were missing, and never retrieved. Two years later, I came home to find the front door ripped out of its frame, drawers all over the floor, and every silver object gone. By the time George got home there were three police cars in the driveway, convincing him that I had been murdered. One police car was the one I had called for, but the rookie cop didn't have the right forms so he phoned for a back-up. In the meantime, a state trooper cruising in the area picked up the call on his radio and joined the party. This was too much for George, and he was on the phone with Security and Surveillance the next day.

We have a simple system, not one of those fancy switchboards, and have had no problems since, except for a couple of times when we set off the alarm accidentally by absentmindedly opening the door before turning the alarm key. Whether the sign on the door is a deterrent or the grapevine has spread the word that we have not replaced our stolen articles, I don't know, but after George died, friends and relatives began hinting that I should have "Life Line," or something similar, in case I fell down in the garden or slipped on the ice going out for the mail. Joan Cross pointed out that I could have it tied in with the security system. So now I have a new item of jewelry, a little button in a pendant that I can wear around my neck.

If I press the button, the security office is notified and they phone me. If I am unable to answer the phone, they call my nearest neighbor who is most likely to be at home, then another neighbor, and then Debbie. If they are unable to rouse any of those, the police are called.

Sounds good. Too good. One cold day, I decided it was time to bring my pickles and jellies into the house from the garage. Having been admonished by George to ALWAYS carry heavy bundles close to the chest in kindness to my back, I made several trips hugging a rough wicker basket full of jars. Shortly after I was back in the house to stay, there was a frantic pounding on the front door.

"Are you all right?"

I went to the door and found an excited young woman.

"On my car radio it said that the police have called the Richmond Rescue to a house on Nashville Road, one mile east of Brown's Trace. That's you!"

As I stood open-mouthed, we heard the wail of a siren coming nearer and soon, with lights flashing, a big red and white ambulance roared into the drive. Out jumped four smartly-uniformed attendants, two men and two women, who came running to the door and stopped abruptly when they saw the victim both vertical and vocal. I reached into my blouse and pulled out the small offending alarm button. The phone rang. It was Clara Manor, the first person on my list, who said they had just returned from grocery shopping and heard on their scanner that a Richmond Rescue ambulance was headed in my direction. Neither Claudia Bechard, the second name on my list, nor Debbie had been at home when they had been called.

The rescue squad was very nice about it, assuring me that they were not disappointed to have their equipment not used. The man in charge suggested that I might try wearing the pendant hanging down in back. I privately thought that if I were as amply endowed as Dolly Parton, the alarm button would have been more safely hidden.

By coincidence, the notice of the annual fund drive for the Richmond Rescue came the next day. I sent a check. If I'm going to wrench those volunteers away from their jobs, into their uniforms, and onto a wild goose chase, the least I can do is cover their mileage.

PIG TALES

The expression "Pigs is Pigs" isn't necessarily true. It wasn't in the book of that name by Ellis Parker Butler, which was popular in the early part of this century. Those prolific creatures were guinea pigs. And do you remember Arnold in "Green Acres?" Anatomically he was a pig, but Hollywood had taught him a lot of parlor tricks.

Pigs have been given a bad rap. They don't deserve it. We kept two pigs each year, except when we were exiled to Massachusetts and Kansas for a while. But now that I am no longer locally known as "the pig lady," my daughter Debbie and her husband, Steve Page, are carrying on the family tradition.

Their first two pigs knew they were pigs, or at least didn't have any delusions that they were anything else. They spent their days inside a well-appointed pig pen at some distance from the house. Having been forewarned by us that piglets have a Houdini-like ability to escape from a conventional pen, Steve had built them a well-barricaded fortress that had a shelter for shade and enough turf to be turned over to a pig's heart's content. They spent seven months in active consumption for themselves, and then were tucked away in the freezer for active consumption by the Page family.

That's the predictable pattern, but anyone who has raised pigs knows that pigs aren't always predictable.

Two years later they decided to try pigs again. They got two piglets that were really too small to leave Mama, and one of them didn't make it. The Page family, feeling sorry for the lonely survivor, named Billy Bob, spent a lot of quality time with him, with the result of Billy Bob thinking that this was the way life should be. He would manage to dig his way out of his enclosure, and would twinkle up to the house on his little tiptoes looking for entertainment.

To the piglet's delight, Muff, Morgan's golden retriever, welcomed this new playmate, and they rolled on the ground together and chased each other like puppies. When you drove into their yard, both Muff and Billy Bob greeted you enthusiastically, squealing and wagging their tails. When Debbie and Morgan went for a walk, Muff and Billy Bob trotted along too, a big bushy golden and a very small round pink piglet. There was no danger that Billy Bob would run away. He would have happily moved right into the house and slept with Morgan.

The problem was that he was soon rearranging the yard to his tastes. Piglets don't stay the size of Christopher Robin's friend. They grow rapidly and their chief delight in life, after eating, is rooting with that amazingly efficient hard rubber snout. It was cute at first, but soon he began bulldozing huge swaths across the lawn and turning over the vegetable garden just for exercise.

Another anxiety was that Billy Bob's function was supposed to be to produce food, and if he became too much a member of the family, how could they face the pork chops and bacon?

So they began weaning him away from the bosom of the family and reprogramming him as a pig. He adjusted to his new role with equanimity. I doubt if they could have brought themselves to butcher him at home, but it is surprising how little the neat packages of pork, wrapped for the freezer, resemble a live pig. Still, I'm glad they have pictures of him in his halcyon days. Their Christmas card that year shows the family posing together on their front walk. Steve, Debbie, and Muff are wearing dark glasses. Billy Bob and Morgan are bright-eyed and smiling at the camera.

The next year, Steve built a new pig pen tucked halfway into the woods for a combination of shade and sunshine. The two new pigs thrived, and once again Steve had to face the job of loading them into the truck. Pig loading is a sometime thing. Sometimes it goes smoothly. Sometimes it is an exercise in utter frustration. I used to fancy myself as an expert pig loader, but what red-blooded American son-in-law wants to be guided through pig loading by his mother-in-law? To the surprise of both the pigs and Steve, the two large porkers trotted right up into the truck as if they were going to enter the pig race at the fair. He was so delighted that he took a large marker and wrote "Racing Pigs" across the side of the crate.

The loading was done with such dispatch that he figured he had time for errands on the way. He stopped at one store, and when he came out he found a little circle of people around the truck. "Are they really racing pigs?" they asked. Steve just smiled and patted the crate proudly. At the next stop, the pigs again drew an admiring audience. Steve and the pigs grunted graciously and took off for the abatoir in a rosy glow.

Last year Steve set the date full of confidence. I'll let him tell you in his own words, written in the middle of a sleepless night and presented to his mother-in-law.

Cool, wet September weather turned Venus and Pluto's diggings into a slurry of waste and swill. It was time to send these piggies to market. Unlike last year's tenants, Link and Hogthrob, they were deprived of socializing, such as playing with the dogs, family walks, and appearing in the local Fourth of July parade. They were extremely perplexed and wary about any intrusion into their domestic scene. I took the afternoon off from work to allow plenty of time for a relaxed loading and transport to Hyde Park. I motivated them by food deprivation for a day, slid the ramp from the back of the truck into the pen, sprinkled it liberally with gourmet pig chow, and stood by to see them unwittingly cooperate in their own demise. They thought NOT! Venus was interested in eating, but only as far as her forefeet would take her up the ramp. No amount of cajoling could convince her of my need to get on down the road for a two o'clock appointment. After half an hour of unsuccessful attempts at persuasion, it was time for decisive action. In the immortal words of Ross Perot, "Talk is cheap. Get

81

the job done." So with Venus halfway up the ramp, I conjured up images of my high school days as a football linebacker, and grabbed both ears most firmly. Well, they aren't just ears. They are alarm sensors for the most blood-curdling and hysterical screaming. I was able to "coax" Venus into the back of the pickup, but convincing her to stay there was another matter. I was flipped over onto my head into the waste- and feed-littered bed of the truck, barking my shin and puncturing my arm and ego. She easily evaded my open-field tackle and deftly bolted through the flimsy barricade I'd erected to contain her while I invited Pluto to join her. With blood pressure and frustration soaring, the obvious way to spell relief was to kick the pig, who was now enjoying the new smells outside the pen. My mightiest kick to her left buttock was rewarded with absolutely no reaction, not the slightest movement or whimper.

I realized that I needed to call in the heavy artillery, in the form of my neighbor, Jim McCullough, a native Vermonter wise in the ways of deceiving pigs. Jim sensed the anxiety in my voice and graciously dropped what he was doing.

Jim's opening move was to feign an air of studied indifference of any urgency to get to market, and to infuse the atmosphere with a yoga-like transcendental calm. Venus ambled back into the pen with her own air of studied indifference. Back to square one: replace the ramp, sprinkle it with pig chow, and implore them calmly to walk up the ramp. Half an hour later, no action. We unbolted the feed trough, filled it with feed, and placed it in the rear of the truck. They ignored it, and ravenously attacked the mixture of swill, mud, and waste where the trough had been. Our advances spurned, Jim and I concluded that the bum's rush was in order. Positioned on opposite sides of the ramp, Jim, weighing in at 175 pounds, and I, weighing in at 195 pounds, each grabbed an ear of Pluto, weighing in at 225 pounds. In spite of the high-volume shrieking pig distress horn, we placed mind and matter over pig, and won!

One down and one to go. With Pluto distracted by a bowl of feed in the truck, efforts now focused on Venus, lured to the ramp by the sounds of Pluto's lip smacking. Jim and I applied the bum's rush again. Success! A nifty takedown of the ramp. But before the crate was closed up, Pluto burst through the crate door and was off to greener pastures in the wide open spaces. Attempts at tackling left us empty-handed and sucking wind. Jim stooped to new levels by suggesting that we use his front-end loader for softening up the pigs by dumping a load of stones on them, and then lifting them into the pickup.

We have been at this together now for over two hours, resulting in two heavily-soiled, frustrated humans and two free and happy pigs. Next goal: return the pigs to their pen. Marshalling all our remaining patience, we try to entice Venus and Pluto back into their pen with food and kind words. Eventually, they agreed to return.

Needless to say, the pigs were not showered with affection for the next few days as Steve and I licked our wounds. Then came a flash of inspiration: a pig condo! Seventy-five dollars worth of materials and a half-day of cabinet-level carpentry resulted in a home any pig might lust for, complete with a fool-proof guillotine-style front door and skids underneath for mobility.

Once more with an air of complete indifference, I placed the condo adjacent to the pigpen, furnished it lavishly with bedding, water, and food, propped open the front door, and left to do other chores.

Half an hour later I returned. There stood Debbie and Morgan (returning from a bike ride), admiring the new condo and the two pigs INSIDE it! A quick exchange of silent signals, and the door was quietly lowered behind Pluto's curly tail, not a shriek, not a whimper. CASE CLOSED!

ROCKS

Between a rock and a hard place is a chronic location for most of us in Vermont. We still have both mill stones and mile stones. In fact, the mill stone from the mill that was on our land 150 years ago is firmly wedged between a rock and a hard place in our brook, just above the waterfall. It is a handsome artifact, and visitors often suggest that we bring it up from the brook and turn it into a doorstep. They don't elaborate on how we could get any heavy equipment down the rough 250-yard path that drops seventy-five feet from the level of the house to the level of the brook. But we've never wanted to move it. When the children were small they liked to sit on it and dangle their small feet in the hole in the middle where the water rushed under the stone, a kind of cool whirlpool foot bath on a hot summer day.

But that's not the only rock on our place, not by a long shot. On the grassy flat near the pool there is a big old boulder, dropped off by some receding glacier. Our children called it the Dressing Rock because it was big enough to modestly conceal several people while they changed from work clothes to bathing suits. When Debbie was about four, she wasn't sure why anyone felt the need to hide, but wanted to imitate the older children. So she would take off her shorts and shirt behind the rock, put on a bathing cap, and then run happily naked into the water.

The rest of our land is full of rocks too, like most of Vermont. In the garden is the most predictable perennial crop. How the subsoil can shove up and extrude such a crop of rocks every spring is a continuing mystery. I toss out most of them, but some are useful to anchor that porous cover Remay, black plastic, or the Sunday *New York Times*, which I put around the tomato plants as mulch and weed suppressors. We probably have the most literate garden in Jericho.

I tried to bribe my grandson Patrick into helping me in the garden when he was small. I offered a penny a stone, but I failed to designate size, so when he gathered handfuls of one-inch pebbles, I could see he was more of an entrepreneur than I. Fortunately his boredom preceded my bankruptcy.

There are remnants of old stone walls on our land so moss-covered and sunken that they no longer serve the dual purpose of keeping cattle in and disposing of rocks large enough to trip the plow. It was a while before I knew that a "stun boat" is a flat platform dragged across the fields by horses. The farmer pried out the "stuns" and loaded them on the barge to be carried to the edge of the field, where they would spend the next hundreds of years as a wall. "Good fences make good neighbors," and a good stone wall shows that the neighbor was a skilled craftsman. There is a real art in building a stone wall that will last. I know two men who, over the protests of their backs, make a hobby out of constructing stone walls. They are not farmers. One is a pediatrician and the other is an engineer. But they are skilled craftsmen who enjoy placing the stones in alignment to endure.

We had a problem rock in the front lawn, about a foot in diameter and protruding six inches above ground. George went at it with a crowbar, forgetting about the tip of the iceberg theory. The contest between George's determination and the rock's tenacity lasted a whole day. When the irresistible force won out over the immoveable object, the resulting crater was far more of a problem than the rock had ever been.

The Lord's Prayer Rock in Bristol is a testament to one man's respect for a rock. The boulder has the entire Lord's Prayer inscribed on it. Whether the help of the Lord was invoked before or after contact with the rock is unknown.

When we moved to Kansas, we were surprised to find that rocks were highly esteemed. Artificial rocks were sold in garden nurseries for rock gardens. George dreamed of filling our truck with Vermont rocks when we came back to Jericho for the summer and taking them back to Kansas for sale.

But I wouldn't want to part with Vermont's rocks. They are part of our character and our ultimate refuge. "Rock of Ages cleft for me. Let me hide myself in Thee."

JERICHO'S HAUNTED HOUSE

The barn and space behind Lil and Gerry Desso's store in Jericho Center was overflowing with spooks and spirits on Halloween. The visible ones were evil and terrifying, but the good ones had been hard at work for a week building this house of many mansions. Ten years ago Karen Desso had the inspiration and talked her parents into a show that now has fifteen skits and booths. Admission is free, and all the participants are volunteers. They include children, teenagers, and a cross-section of neighbors, who spend the rest of the year as butchers, bakers, and candlestick makers.

This year the guests were greeted and entertained by devils, who stamped their hands with a "Lilosaurus" insignia to qualify for entrance. In past years, anywhere from seven hundred to nine hundred people have lined up to wait an hour or more to creep through the dark passageway into the witch's den, where the witch was stirring a cauldron of toads and mice for her children's supper. Then on to the Miss Halloween contest, where poor Miss Halloween was finally spirited off by a werewolf. The skeleton, a real one, was next, and then a cooking class, where repulsive ingredients were brewing as a feast for the Grim Reaper.

"Gerryassic Park" was the site of a spooky laboratory where dinosaur eggs hatched. A volcano reminiscent of Mt. St. Helens extended into Elsie and Win Smith's backyard next door. Thumping and grunting emanating from the next enclosure turned out to be the gyrations of Sumo wrestlers, who made up in enthusiasm what they lacked in girth.

Goldilocks didn't find three bears eating her porridge, but three monsters, who ghoulishly served up her head on a platter. Of course, there had to be a menacing Dracula; in fact, it was rumored that Kay Howard was such a convincing vampire that it has become her annual role in the show.

A dark, enclosed hut was inhabited by head hunters who were actually students from the Community Service Class at Mt. Mansfield High School and welcomed this unusual form of community service with glee. It is an interesting commentary that teenage vandalism has become noticeably absent in Jericho since so many in that age group have taken on the responsibility of planning and performing in this Halloween party.

The Wizard used strange lighting effects to make a person appear and disappear, and to dissolve a whole face into a single eye. Shrunken heads adorned the walls of the last booth. In the dim light, they were realistic enough to make you think fondly of the real world you hoped was still outside. But you were not released that simply. You had to crawl out through a curtain, almost on your hands and knees to finally get a glimpse of the comforting village green.

For several years, Gerry Desso and assorted relatives have taken time off from work to erect the walls and partitions of this extravaganza. This is the last year that the Desso's will host the Haunted House. It has become so popular that next year it will move across the street to the Community Center.

Community spirit may be dying out in some Vermont towns, but it is alive and well among the skeletons and hobgoblins of Jericho Center.

SOLITUDE AND LONELINESS

Don't let a crossword puzzle convince you that loneliness is a synonym for solitude. Solitude is freedom to shape an hour or a day without pressure from job, family, or community. Loneliness is when you feel that you are unneeded and unrecognized. Solitude is a vacation from a demanding job. Loneliness is no job at all.

When each of us is plunged into widowhood or retirement, the framework of our life is suddenly changed. "People who have regular jobs can have no idea of just this problem of ordering a day that has no pattern imposed on it from without," May Sarton wrote in *Journal of Solitude*.

Certainly no healthy person wants to consider retirement or widowhood as leftover time to kill. The autumn of life, as in the autumn of the year, can be either ripe maturity or incipient decline. Why nursing homes depress us is that, in spite of the efforts of staff and family, the pervading atmosphere is that their patients no longer serve a useful purpose.

Each of us has experienced loneliness at different times. The small child in a doctor's office, undressed and in a strange environment, who asks "May I hold my shoes?" wants to retain his identity. When Patty completed her flight training and was told to take the plane up alone, she asked if she could take her instructor's jacket up with her.

I have been loneliest in a hotel room in a foreign country, even though I was not alone, because I had no function there. I was not useful in any way, except to help the local economy by paying for room and meals.

Solitude is positive because it is a reward, a privilege, an escape from routine. Time unbounded is hard to handle. One winter George and I visited four different couples in Florida. All had been active, professional people involved in their communities in the North. But two of the couples now spent most of their time developing little schedules to convince themselves that they were busy. At specified times they got the paper, took a walk, played bridge, and went grocery shopping. The other two couples gloried in their release from former responsibilities and a harsher climate, but they were active in volunteer jobs and courses in painting and music.

Dr. John Bland, a retired professor of rheumatology at UVM College of Medicine, emphasizes that weight-bearing exercise keeps muscles, tendons, and bones in good shape. You need that pressure for physical well-being, and we need reasonable pressure and expectations for emotional health as well.

An unlimited vacation is no vacation at all. It becomes a burden. The well-earned reward of solitude is the antithesis of loneliness.

THE BARE BONES
OF NOVEMBER

November is a Monday morning kind of month. October is an extravaganza of color, when you drive through golden tree tunnels of sugar maples, and every hillside is a kaleidoscope of saffron, garnet, apricot, and scarlet. By November the radiance has gone. November is Lent after Mardi Gras. She has taken off her October finery and left it lying on the ground, where it glows briefly like an oriental rug but soon fades to a moist brown carpet.

There is still some gold to be found in these hills. The tamaracks come into their own, tall spires of gold contrasting with the dark evergreens. Even a few late dandelions shine out in the fields, but the time between the falling leaves and the falling snow is painted from a somber palette.

November is a month of gathering. Wood is to be stacked and the last root crops of carrots and beets are to be dug up. The country houses are to be banked with evergreen boughs, bags of leaves, or tar paper. The farm wife takes pleasure in her shelves of pickles, jellies, and canned fruits and vegetables. Some of them may now be in the freezer, but for me, a stack of packages in the freezer is not as visually satisfying as the rows of multicolored jars.

Thanksgiving is a gathering of people. No holiday pulls the American family together more than Thanksgiving. Not even Christmas. As children get older they want to have Christmas in their own homes, but they go back to their parents' house for Thanksgiving. It has to be a feast. Even the apartment dweller without a garden feels compelled to roast a turkey and, perhaps, considers making cranberry sauce from scratch.

The country dweller pulls out all the culinary stops for the Thanksgiving feast. It is a time to celebrate abundance. Stuffed turkey, squash, potatoes, cranberry sauce, and rolls fill the table, with pumpkin and mince pie for dessert, even though half the family really would prefer ice cream. Traditional food preferences are argued and resolved. My father felt that creamed onions were essential. My mother favored a moist dressing of bread cubes, celery, and onions. My mother-in-law made a dry bread crumb dressing with sausage. There are families who insist on oyster stuffing even if they don't really like oysters. And in the South, cornbread dressing is as ubiquitous as candied sweet potatoes.

Even though I do not share the November enthusiasm for hunting and football, there are some small pleasures that assuage my November megrims. The bugs are gone! From black flies in June to wasps in September, I applaud their absence. Perhaps the best thing about November is that now you can see the true shape of a wineglass elm, or the sturdiness of an oak, or the gnarled, uplifted arms of an apple tree that have been hidden in foliage. Lights from distant houses shine at nightfall. Shape has become more important than color. The bare bones of a tree reveal its unique personality. We need November to understand essential shapes that are camouflaged by leaves and flowers. Would I be so exhilarated by the first crocus or fiddlehead fern had I not lived with the brown grass and matted leaves?

In spite of my lack of enthusiasm for November's shortening days, I could not welcome the winter snow or the miraculous resurrection of spring if I had not known the stark reality of November.

THE PERFECT
CHRISTMAS TREE

Lewis Hill, in his book *Fetched Up Yankee*, says "Nature abhors a perfect Christmas tree." He's right. Most of them growing in the wild have had to adapt to local pressure, opting for survival rather than symmetry. Of course, the specimen chosen each year for the White House or Radio City comes close, but there is something to be said for the slight imperfections that give a Christmas tree, or a person, individuality. Who wants perfection anyway? Cindy Crawford is no less beautiful because she has a mole at the corner of her mouth. In fact, it has become a trademark and widely copied. As long ago as the seventeenth century, Robert Herrick wrote:

A sweet disorder in the dress...
Do more bewitch me, than when art
Is too precise in every part.

And I feel the same way about Christmas trees, which is a good thing, because in my experience there is no such thing as a perfect Christmas tree.

Now that they are grown commercially with plenty of space between trees, they are more symmetrical than those found in the wild. Of course, if you want to settle for an artificial tree you can have one of monochromatic emerald green that presents the same fullness from every angle and has indefinite longevity. It's convenient: no shedding, no mess, but, alas, with none of the wonderful fragrance that is the essence of Christmas.

When our children were small, we rarely bought a Christmas tree. We got into the truck, drove out to Jericho, staggered up the snowy hillside on our own land looking for the tree of the year. As we spread out in the woods, each member of the family discovered a different tree with merit. Everyone was critical of the other choices. One was too crooked, another was the wrong kind (they were supposed to be spruce or balsam). George groaned when they favored a huge one. The girls moaned that my choice was too small.

The day was always cold. The sun was sinking in a lemon-colored sky. It was slippery underfoot, and George's patience was wearing thin.

"If you don't decide in the next two minutes, I'm going to cut down whatever tree I'm standing near." Of course he didn't mean it. The tree next to him was either a "popple" or a maple, but it did motivate compromise, and a choice was often made because of a fault rather than perfection. One that was too tall would look funny with its top lopped off, but one that was slightly flat in back would fit better against the wall.

So George cut down the tree and carried it back to the truck, and from that moment on it automatically became the most beautiful tree we had ever had. It would have been heresy to call attention to the gap on one side or the slightly crooked trunk. It had become a member of the family, and we were united in our loyalty. Certain rituals had to be observed. The lights had to go on first, a chore I hated because I always ended up with a female plug where I needed a male one. But I was stuck with the job because no one else wanted it, and no ornaments could go on until the lights were in place. There was plenty of help hanging the prettiest ornaments, or the old ones that had sentimental history: one made in school by very small fingers forty years ago, George's rather limp baby shoe donated by his mother, straw ornaments from Scandinavia, and rock-hard ancient marzipan from Germany. George insisted on tinsel which he called "rain." And underneath the tree we placed the beautiful appliqued felt wrap-around skirt made for my sister by her niece, Mrs. Phil Zerega.

When we take out the old decorations, we inevitably unwrap memories of Christmases past: funny ones, wonderful ones, and a few bittersweet times. Perhaps the best Christmas gifts we can give our children and grandchildren this year are not expensive toys or sports equipment, but warm Christmas memories to pack away for future Christmases.

WHAT'S GOOD ABOUT JANUARY?

What's good about January? Not much at first glance. Nobody wants to go back to school or work. Even those New Year's resolutions seem increasingly unrealistic. There's only one holiday, the bittersweet remembrance of Martin Luther King's birthday. While I vacuum up the needles from the Christmas tree, I am not elated by the thought of three and a half more months of winter. Yes, that much more. We live in Vermont, remember, and while we have intimations of Spring in March, she doesn't show her rain-washed face until late April.

But post-Christmas depression is gradually lifted by the return of light. One day, for the first time since mid-December, it is not yet dark at 4:30 in the afternoon. The birds are still active at the feeders, and I can see the ice-encrusted waterfall quite clearly.

"Relieve my languish and restore the light." Three hundred years ago, Samuel Daniel had struggled against those winter blahs.

And two hundred years before that, Bishop Gavin Douglas said "Welcum the lord of lycht and lamp of day."

My spirits rise, and I ferret out those burrowing needles with renewed vigor. There is a light at the end of winter's dark tunnel, and it is growing brighter each day.

Last night's snowfall seems to increase the light, and it presents a clean page for the diary of activity around my house. I rarely see the deer, the snowshoe hare, or the weasel, but they print a story on the fresh snow. The deer has leapt the garden fence, pawed away some snow, and gleaned the few remaining carrot tops. The parsley is nipped close to the ground, but the doe wasn't interested in thyme or catnip. A snowshoe hare's big tracks circle the house and then, frightened by something, perhaps a hawk, bound into the woods in long leaps. A tiny meadow mouse was not so lucky. The minute lacy footprints emerging from a snowbank end in a disturbed area marked only by a drop of blood and a wisp of taupe fur.

Large human footprints march up the driveway right to the house. Who was that? I had no visitors. But they lead to the electric meter on the outside wall. The meter reader. I can tell if the newspaper has been delivered because Donald Howe's car tracks swoop in close to the blue box. A big town truck with wide tires turned into our driveway, backed out, and headed in the other direction. Bob Aiken has already been out running at the edge of the road, and someone else with a dog has walked on the same side. A ruffed grouse has flown down from a wild apple tree and foraged around, leaving her unique tracks, three-toed in front with the little toe in back. The weight of its body pressed the tracks in farther than the dainty prints of the chickadees under the feeder. A woodpecker would have left a different print, with two toes in front and two in back, but my woodpeckers stick to the trees, quite literally, where those two back toes anchor them firmly in position.

I used to love the little footprints Morgan's tiny boots left on the path when he was first walking. Now his twelve-year-old boots are bigger than mine and indistinguishable from Debbie's. A new, exciting message has been left on the path to the garden, prints in a straight line and bigger than a dog's. According to my book it was a wild canine. The outer toe prints are larger. A coyote! Even though my shepherd neighbors don't welcome the coyotes, I wish I had seen him. There is something wonderfully wild about a coyote.

I'll have to wait for the sounds of wildness, the demonic laughter of a loon, or the sleighbell chorus of the Canada geese when they come back north, but I'm glad that wild creatures are living close around me.

The return of light tells me that the geese and the loon will come back. But it will snow again, and the message tape will be wiped clear, ready for a new story to be read tomorrow.

DEEP FREEZE

Winter in Vermont is a Christmas card, with snow-covered evergreens, skiers on the slopes, red barns, and white-steepled churches. But for the year-round Vermonter, winter is also sub-zero temperatures, far-below-zero wind chills, frozen pipes, escalating heating bills, and roads that test your driving skills as well as the tread of your tires.

Winter is a test of faith. If you have always lived in a warm climate and suddenly find yourself in Vermont in February, you will surely think that the world is about to end in ice. How can life in a seed or a hibernating animal survive this deep, penetrating freeze? They can because winter is also a nurturer. Snow is a warm blanket, enabling seeds and many creatures to escape the life-threatening cold.

Sometimes the wind is loud and raucous, with gusts of wind lashing the trees, blowing snow in circles, hissing and spitting. When the temperature drops to zero, the snow squeaks under your boots.

A sound like a pistol shot may be a young maple splitting, and at night the beams and rafters boom ominously in protest. Sometimes the intense cold is as silent as death, aching your forehead, numbing your fingers, motionless, waiting, daring you to challenge its awesome strength. But it is also cleansing, purifying, and humbling. In order to survive, you must believe that the ice on the lake will melt in March, that the chipmunk will peep out of his hole, and that snowdrops will push up through the snow, if only to be covered again. There is an urge to sleep through the winter like the bear and woodchuck, or snooze like the raccoon. You could choose the preferred human form of survival, migrating to a warm climate, but you cannot stop winter in Vermont. Would you know the comfort of coming in to a warm, bright, and fragrant kitchen, or thawing out in front of an open fire, if it was not contrasted to the cold outside? Can you appreciate the warmth of kindness and friendship if you have never been lonely or afraid?

Winter is a test of belief in the great cycles of the year. In spring it is easy to believe in the vitality of a seed. Spring in Vermont is fragile and as shy as a newborn lamb. Summer is an affirmation of belief, to be savored as you pick the crisp pea pods and sun-ripened tomatoes followed by the bonfire of fall. But in summer you need to remember the garden when it was deep in snow with only the taffeta rustle of corn stalks and the click of brittle asparagus ferns shivering in the wind.

And in winter you need to remember that change is eternal, that there is a wholeness in the year. No matter how deep and awesome the cold, beneath the snow and high in the sky the cycle continues. In order to survive we must keep the faith.

WELCOME TO
VERMONT, BUT
PLEASE DON'T STAY!

Many people equate Vermont with Nirvana, a place of escape from the problems of urban life, the promised land flowing with milk and maple syrup.

It's not a new idea. Years ago, Bernard de Voto said that everyone dreams of Vermont as his second home. And George Aiken said, "I'd rather be on the floor of the Town Hall than on the floor of the Senate chamber on the first Tuesday after the first Monday in March."

Of course, Christmas cards, ski posters, and *Vermont Life* advertise the scenic side of our state, and there still exists the myth of the taciturn, honest, independent Vermonter who answers only to Ethan Allen's gods of the hills. He is still here but is outnumbered in the towns and resorts by people "from away."

We too came from away, but we came forty-six years ago, when Vermont welcomed immigrants. It was exporting more young people than it was retaining. I had one foot in the door by virtue of two Vermont great-grandfathers. That has done a lot to remove the stigma of being from New York, Vermont's historical enemy. In many states you will find more transplants than natives. You expect this in California, Florida, or in the Southwest where the climate has lured many retired persons. But Vermont has not been a retirement mecca. Snow and below-zero temperatures have less appeal to senior citizens than sunshine and beaches.

Then who is responding to the siren song of Vermont? Young business people who want to escape from the city, summer people who want to stay year-round, skiers and vacationers who want to turn an avocation into a vocation, artists and writers who hope to live more cheaply than in the city. They come looking for Vermont's rural atmosphere and a simpler life style. But after they have been here a while, they start making "improvements": bigger malls, national bookstores, more sophisticated boutiques. And pretty soon they are remodeling Vermont into a clone of the city or suburb they have left. The very things they came for are not enough on a year-round basis. So it is not surprising that some of us welcome the urbanites as visitors, but hope they will go home before they try to urbanize us.

We don't want more pollution, more traffic, more stores that are owned by absentee conglomerates. We are struggling hard to protect the environment and have led the field in this effort. Desso's Store in Jericho is the heart of the village. It is not a quaint relic with a spittoon and a pot-bellied stove. Lil and Gerry, who speak to everyone who comes into the store, preside over an emporium that has everything from hunting licenses to Ben and Jerry's ice cream. Incidentally, both Ben and Jerry live only a few miles away, and we applaud their community spirit and environmental concern. But Lil has her finger on the pulse of the village, as well as the red emergency phone. Santa Claus visits there every Christmas, and the Desso's put on an elaborate Halloween party for as many as one thousand kids.

We don't want to lose that sense of community. We want to keep what Donna Fitch calls "the feeling of being connected with the land, with our neighbors, with our family, with Vermont."

So if you want to get away from it all, you are welcome to come and be one of us, if you will share our hope of keeping place over people, not people over place. But if you plan to bring the "all" that you want to get away from with you, welcome to Vermont, but please don't stay.